Plant Power Bowls

70 Seasonal Vegan Recipes to **Boost Energy** and Promote Wellness

Sapana Chandra
Creator of ***Real + Vibrant***

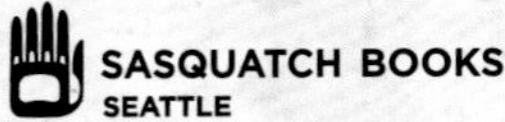

Copyright © 2019 by Sapana Chandra
Real + Vibrant is a registered trademark of Sapana Chandra
Photographs copyright © 2019 by Sapana Chandra

All rights reserved. No portion of this book may be reproduced or utilized in any form, or by any electronic, mechanical, or other means, without the prior written permission of the publisher.

Printed in China

Published by Sasquatch Books

26 25 24 23 22 9 8 7 6 5 4 3 2 1

Editor: Susan Roxborough
Production editor: Rachelle Longé McGhee
Copyeditor: Kirsten Colton
Designer: Bryce de Flamand
All photographs and styling: Sapana Chandra except © iStockphoto.com/natthanim (p. i)
Author photo by David Em (p. viii, endsheet)
Cover stylist: Bridget Meyer

This book is not intended to diagnose, treat, cure, or prevent any disease. Its content should not be considered a substitute for professional medical expertise or treatment.

Library of Congress Cataloging-in-Publication Data is available.

ISBN: 978-1-63217-468-0

Sasquatch Books
1325 Fourth Avenue, Suite 1025
Seattle, WA 98101

SasquatchBooks.com

This book is dedicated to my Instagram community. Thank you for being part of my journey to health, for supporting me every step of the way, and for believing in me. I wouldn't be writing this book if it weren't for you.

And to my parents—my mother, for teaching me about the power of real food, and my father, for reminding me when I had forgotten.

Finally, this book is dedicated to anyone who is struggling with their health and looking to heal. I've been there and understand how difficult it can be. Please know that you are stronger and more resilient than you can ever imagine. I hope this book helps you use the power of real food on your own journey.

Contents

Fall Bowls 87

Winter Bowls 125

My Story

Health is something we often take for granted, until we lose it. I remember the day I lost mine.

It was a sunny afternoon in the spring of 2004. I had joined the corporate world six months earlier, right after graduating with my master's in computer science, and was working at a job I loved.

The pain hit me all at once. The backs of my eyes started aching, and I felt a creeping pressure rise up my face. The sunlight I had been enjoying all morning suddenly felt too bright, and the clicking of the keyboard from my coworker sitting next to me sounded too loud. Then I felt the sharpest jab in my head, and the throbbing began. I closed my eyes, but that only made me feel nauseated. I put my head down on my desk, trying to block out the fluorescent lighting, hallway conversations, people's footsteps. Every sound, every light, every movement felt magnified. And the pain was only getting worse.

What was happening to me? This pain was like nothing I had ever felt before. A coworker dropped me off at my apartment since I wasn't in a condition to drive. Hours later, I was lying under the covers of my bed, holding my head, unable to fall asleep, with tears streaming down my face from the intensity of it all.

When my physician returned my call, he listened to my symptoms and finally said, "Well, it sounds like you just had your first migraine."

That moment was the beginning of a long journey to find help. Over the next decade, I tried one treatment after another, one prescription drug after another. I would frequently have no choice but to cancel plans with friends, miss work, and avoid anything that could possibly trigger a migraine.

As my quality of life started to deteriorate, my search for help grew more intense. I was willing to try anything, from traditional Western to alternative medicine. I had the desire to live a healthy life, to find a treatment that worked, and while I was getting nowhere close to either, I never lost hope.

One night a few years ago, I found myself watching a documentary—Joe Cross's *Fat, Sick, and Nearly Dead.* I was incredibly moved by his transformation. By juicing fruits and vegetables, Joe lost over a hundred pounds and got off all of his prescription medications, completely rebooting his life. I immediately ordered my first juicer. I soon started juicing, blending smoothies, and cooking homemade meals again. I kept it simple and combined fresh, seasonal ingredients for maximum nutrients and flavor. My confidence in the kitchen grew, my migraines disappeared, and my energy soared.

Months into my new lifestyle, I got a phone call that changed my life. My dad had gone into sudden cardiac arrest after a massive heart attack and had been rushed into an emergency quadruple bypass surgery. It was the beginning of a long road to recovery for him and the beginning of a new career for me. I found myself reading book after book about heart disease and wellness. The more I read, the more I realized that I wanted to help him, the rest of my family, my friends, and everyone else I could reach to learn about the power of real food.

They say you find your strengths through life's biggest adversities. What I learned from my own health issues and from witnessing the sickness of the most important people in my life is just how precious our health is. I saw firsthand what losing it did to my own life and those closest to me. I believe that better health and wellness should be accessible to everyone. A big step toward that is eating real, whole food that makes you feel vibrant from the inside out.

I want to emphasize that I'm not here to push a specific diet on you. While all the recipes are plant based, this book welcomes all types of eaters. Regardless of what dietary theory you associate yourself with, this book will help you incorporate more plants into your meals. I've been a vegetarian all my life, and today I enjoy a primarily plant-based diet because that's what makes me feel my best right now. However, I also believe that our dietary needs are as unique as we are, and they often shift throughout our lifetime.

Health is not about eating perfectly at every meal of every day. We could be eating all the kale and spinach in the world, but it won't make a significant difference until we've addressed other important aspects that may be weighing heavily on us or preventing us from living our best life. Health is about sticking to those seemingly small habits that pay dividends: surrounding ourselves with uplifting people, exercising regularly, sleeping well, choosing positive thoughts, living in a supportive environment, and so much more. It means taking the time and effort to assess and focus on those other important aspects of our lives on a regular basis.

It's when we bring awareness and effort into our daily lives that transformation occurs, and we start to see big changes in our health and life.

If you are currently struggling with your health, I assure you that you are not alone. I know all too well how hard it is to be optimistic when our bodies start failing us, to not give up hope. No matter where you are in your health journey—whether you feel vibrant or not—know that you can take the first step to changing its trajectory at this moment. If I can do it, so can you.

Wishing you real and vibrant health,

How to Use This Book

Buddha bowls, often referred to as hippie bowls or macro bowls, are filling dishes full of clean, whole foods, including leafy greens, raw or roasted vegetables, beans or lentils, grains, and healthy fats. They include toppings such as nuts, seeds, and dressings for added flavor and texture.

In my experience, bowls have been a simple and sustainable way of eating more whole foods at home. I consider them go-to meals when I don't have much time to spend in the kitchen. I simply look in my refrigerator and pair ingredients that taste good together. With bowls, I can combine raw ingredients from the garden with leftovers from the refrigerator, keeping my meals interesting without too much effort. The possibilities are essentially endless and go well beyond the recipes in this book.

There are seventy plant-powered recipes included here to help you reconnect with real food. While each recipe makes two single-serving bowls, it can be reduced by half for one or doubled for four. I'll often cook more than I need and store the leftovers in a lidded glass container for grabbing on the go. Or I'll prepare ingredients that require more time—roasting sweet potatoes, making cauliflower rice, chopping up greens—at the beginning of the week, then store each ingredient separately to use as needed. Essentially my fridge and pantry transform into a vibrant buffet where I pick and choose what I want to make a satisfying bowl.

This is the cookbook I wish I'd had when I first started spending more time making my own meals—one that would easily help me prepare delicious dishes aligned with the seasons, allowing me to feel my very best any time of the year. For this reason, I have organized the book by season so that you, too, can fuel your body with ingredients that will leave you feeling vibrant and energized.

Think of these bowls as a starting point. My hope is that these recipes give you the confidence to create meals that fuel you, leaving you nourished and empowering you to reclaim your health.

Start simple, with small, achievable goals. When I first started cooking at home again, my goal was to master a couple of recipes per month. I picked two basic ones that I felt sure I could make and would enjoy eating. I made each of the recipes as often as I could during that month—enough to get comfortable and feel confident. Soon I had a repertoire that I felt great about, and naturally I started creating my own dishes.

Extra Dressing

The dressing recipes in this book make enough for two bowls. However, you can always prepare a greater quantity or make the dressing a few days in advance and then store the extra in the refrigerator. Most will keep for three to five days, although the vinaigrettes may be stored for up to two weeks.

Essential Tools

In this section, you'll find my suggestions for basic tools, appliances, and gadgets that help run your plant-powered kitchen. I didn't purchase all of these items in a single day, month, or even year, as that would have been overwhelming and pricey. Each item was an investment I made as my skills, enthusiasm, and needs progressed in the kitchen. As you spend more time making your own meals and figuring out what works best for you, you'll be able to determine what set of tools enhances your own cooking experience.

Bench scraper: I use this handy tool to scoop up ingredients I've sliced, chopped, or minced. It also works nicely for plating the bowls in sections.

Blender: While a high-speed blender isn't a requirement for any of the recipes in this cookbook, it is hands down my favorite gadget in the kitchen. It is my most expensive device, but it's also one I would suggest prioritizing over anything else. I use my high-speed blender at least once a day—and often multiple times—to blend smoothies, beverages, soups, dressings, sauces, nut butters, ice cream, and so much more. The two most trusted brands are Vitamix and Blendtec, with comparable features—you can't go wrong with either.

Bowls: Have a variety of bowls that are large and deep, able to hold three to four cups of food comfortably. I prefer seven- to nine-inch-wide bowls made of ceramic or porcelain. Most of my bowls are white, off-white, and shades of gray to keep the focus on the food. You could use similar bowls or use colorful ones if you prefer.

Soaking Nuts & Dates

Soaking nuts in water before using them in a recipe—especially a dressing or smoothie—will help plump them up and make them easier to blend. In addition, there are a number of health benefits to soaking nuts, including making the digestion process easier. Simply soak the nuts in room-temperature water for a minimum of thirty minutes. If you'd like them to sprout, soak for at least eight hours. Rinse well and drain them before using.

Likewise, when using dates for the ice-cream recipes in this book (see Treat Bowls on page 163), it's important to first soak them in a bowl of room-temperature water for at least thirty minutes to soften them. (Drain fully afterward.) Doing so allows them to blend with other ingredients more easily and creates a creamier texture. If you have a high-speed blender, you can skip this step, though it doesn't hurt.

Chef's knife: Owning a good-quality chef's knife can transform your experience in the kitchen. Learning how to handle your knife correctly will make prepping ingredients quick and so much more enjoyable. There are tons of resources online that teach you how to properly use a knife—I strongly recommend checking them out so you can master this essential skill.

Cutting board: I have a thick wooden cutting board that's large enough to hold all the ingredients I need to prepare. I take care of it by washing it as soon as I'm done with it and oiling it on a regular basis to prevent it from becoming dry and brittle. I avoid plastic cutting boards altogether.

Fine-mesh strainer or sieve: I use mine to rinse grains and strain juices. It also works well for sifting cocoa powder or flour.

Food processor: While a food processor is not essential, it is a rather useful gadget for making dips, batters, salsas, cauliflower rice, bliss balls, and so much more. A mini processor can be especially handy for small batches.

Glass containers with lids: Invest in a set with various sizes to store both leftovers and ingredients you've prepared in advance. They make it easy to find what you're looking for in the refrigerator and are a breeze to clean. I avoid plastic as much as possible for both environmental and health reasons.

Glass jars: Having a dozen or so canning jars, such as Weck brand, to store dried beans, nuts and seeds, and other key ingredients can help organize your pantry, so you can easily see what you have.

Graters: Having a few different types of graters can make ingredient prep much more convenient. I use a box grater for grating carrots, zucchini, and cauliflower. A Microplane allows you to zest citrus and finely grate ginger or whole spices, such as nutmeg. A mandoline is nice to have for thinly slicing vegetables but isn't essential.

Ice-cream maker: While the ice-cream recipes in this book all require an ice-cream maker, you may decide to pass on this slightly bulky machine. However, if you have a sweet tooth and crave frozen treats, investing in one may be a great idea!

Nontoxic parchment paper or silicone mats: Parchment paper is a great nonstick liner that makes it easy to clean up after you're done; silicone mats are a more expensive but reusable alternative. I use parchment whenever I roast any vegetables.

Peeler: While I enjoy eating most of my vegetables with the skin, as it contains nutrients and fiber, there are times when I may want to remove it. A peeler is also great for making vegetable "ribbons" for added texture and aesthetic appeal.

Pressure cooker or Instant Pot: This is another nice-to-have appliance that will make cooking more efficient, especially when batch cooking beans or grains, making soups, or steaming vegetables. It cuts down cooking time significantly.

Salad spinner or colander: Since most of my meals include leafy greens, using a salad spinner removes excess water and helps keep the leaves crisp. Alternatively, you can use a colander to rinse and dry your greens, though it won't dry them as well as a spinner.

Spiralizer: This tool turns vegetables into "noodles." You can spiralize zucchini, sweet potatoes, carrots, or just about any vegetables large and wide enough to fit into the device. A julienne peeler is an alternative option—just be careful not to hurt yourself using it, as the blades are very sharp.

Stocking the Pantry

Stocking up on essentials can make the biggest difference when choosing between a home-cooked meal and takeout. When you have the ingredients you need to make a quick meal at your fingertips, you're less likely to reach for the alternative. The list below outlines some of the ingredients I keep in my home at all times. They make creating meals made with whole foods convenient while also giving me a variety of options to choose from.

Why No Soy?

Despite this being a plant-based book, I don't include soy ingredients other than the occasional edamame, tamari, or miso. There's enough controversy over soy's effect on health and how it is processed that I mostly leave it out of my own diet. It's up to you to decide whether you want to add tofu or tempeh to your bowls for more protein and variety.

Apple cider vinegar (ACV): Made through a fermentation process, ACV is high in phosphorus, magnesium, potassium, and calcium. ACV supports the digestive and immune systems, among other benefits. It's important to purchase raw, unpasteurized apple cider vinegar with the mother, the bacteria that helps create the vinegar, so that you're getting the full benefits of ACV.

Nut butters: These are great for topping breakfast bowls; adding to smoothies; using in dressings, sauces, and baked goods; and eating alone or as a snack. Some delicious options include almond butter, peanut butter, cashew butter, hazelnut butter, and sunflower butter. You can purchase nut butters at the store or make your own at home (see page 188 for instructions).

Nuts: I usually have almonds, cashews, pecans, walnuts, pistachios, macadamia nuts, Brazil nuts, and pine nuts on hand at pretty much all times. Since nuts can be pricey and will go rancid over time, I usually pick up the amount I need for just the coming month from the bulk section of the store. I keep them in airtight glass jars to maintain freshness. Storing them in the fridge or freezer can further help prevent deterioration due to light and heat exposure. Unless you have a high-speed blender, I recommend soaking nuts before using them in dressings (see page xiv for instructions).

Oils: Avocado oil is mostly flavorless and can handle higher heats than more traditional cooking oils. It has a smoke point of 520 degrees F, making it perfect for roasting. For that reason, it's the primary oil used in this cookbook. Coconut oil is another great option, with a smoke point of 350 degrees F, which is useful for sautéing and baking, though it can have a strong coconut flavor. Cold-pressed extra-virgin olive oil is good for salad dressings or anything that doesn't require high heat, as too much will turn it rancid. Toasted sesame oil is a common finishing oil in Asian cuisine and has a nutty flavor.

Salt: Fine sea salt is a terrific option to use for everyday cooking. Salting preferences vary from person to person, so for that reason, most of the recipes in this book indicate a moderate measure of salt and direct you to season "to taste" as a general guideline.

Seeds: Seeds add not only flavor and texture but also countless nutrients. Some of my favorites include pepitas (pumpkin seeds), hemp, chia, flax, sunflower, sesame, and poppy.

Spices: All the spices used in this book can be found at most grocery stores. I prefer regularly purchasing smaller amounts of spices from the bulk section of a natural food store, where I know they are rotated frequently and are therefore fresher. I transfer my spices to glass containers when I get home and add the purchase date with a marker to keep track of their age. Some places allow you to bring your own jars and fill them up, cutting down on plastic waste.

Sweeteners: Medjool dates and pure maple syrup are my go-to sweeteners. Dates provide fiber, energy, and essential minerals. I enjoy using them in my smoothies and desserts or as a snack. If you're planning to use them in smoothies and don't own a high-speed blender, be sure to soak them in water first so they soften up a bit (see the sidebar on page xiv). Maple syrup contains antioxidants and is an excellent natural sugar source. I enjoy using it in small amounts as a replacement for refined options.

Tahini: This paste, made from sesame seeds, can be purchased or made at home (see page 189 for instructions).

My Top Prep Tips

The most valuable lesson I've learned when it comes to making healthy choices is being prepared. If you leave it up to chance to find a meal that will energize you, you might find yourself disappointed. A little preparation goes a long way. My best pieces of advice for cooking from this book are:

- Visit your local farmers' market every week and seek out the featured seasonal picks.
- Find out which days your neighborhood grocery store receives its produce deliveries and prioritize the freshest ingredients possible.
- When shopping for fruits and vegetables, buy exactly what you'll need for the next few days, so you don't end up composting what you don't use.
- Spend an hour or two prepping what you bring home to save time later: roast vegetables, batch cook grains and beans, wash and chop raw vegetables, and make dressings or nut butter.
- Keep your pantry well organized, with like ingredients grouped together for easy access.
- Clean up as you cook, for efficiency (and sanity!): wipe up messes immediately, put away ingredients as soon as you finish with them, and rinse out pots and pans once cooled.
- Finally, turn on some music and enjoy the process of putting together a dish that will fill you up while improving your health.

The Formula: Designing Your Own Bowl

Once you've mastered a few of the recipes in this book, you may eventually decide you want to branch out into your own combinations or just modify some of mine. Here's how you can create a power bowl unique to you:

1 Start by choosing a bowl that can hold your entire meal. I have a number of bowls in various sizes, but my go-to is usually an eight-inch bowl that can hold three to four cups of food.

2 Add leafy greens, such as spinach, spring mix, kale, arugula, romaine, or chard.

3 Add grains or pseudo-grains, such as quinoa, rice, millet, or farro.

Note

This is a general template, so feel free to get creative and do what works for you based on your dietary preferences.

4

Add proteins, such as chickpeas, beans, lentils, or edamame.

5

Add healthy fats, such as avocado, nuts, and seeds.

7

Top it off with a flavorful dressing, sauce, or pesto.

6

Add cooked or raw fruits and vegetables.

Spring Bowls

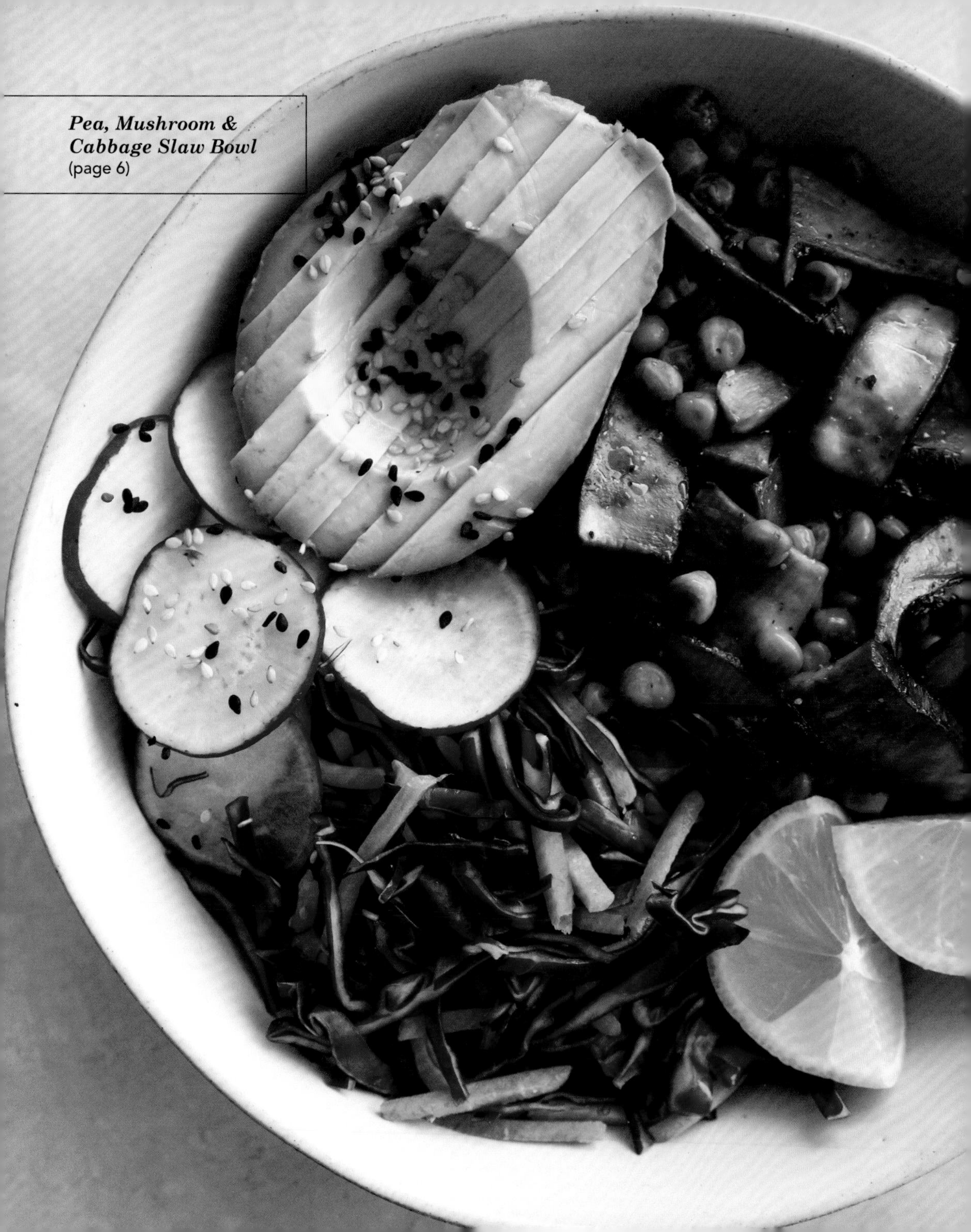

Pea, Mushroom & Cabbage Slaw Bowl
(page 6)

Spring is a time of renewal, of saying goodbye to the old and opening up to the new. The days are a little longer, the air a little warmer, and new life is popping up everywhere. Letting go of the things in our lives that no longer serve us—whether they be relationships that drain us or excess items that create clutter in our homes—can be challenging but is always rewarding.

With this shedding of the heaviness of winter and all of its comfort-driven eating, we get to welcome the spring harvest. It brings us green vegetables of every shade to detoxify our bodies and help us feel lighter from within. It's my favorite time to crowd out any unhealthy habits that may have taken root and swing back into a cleaner eating routine.

With farmers' markets opening up again and fresh produce readily available, spring is one of the easiest times of the year to start incorporating more plants into your diet. Asparagus, peas, fennel, radishes, and spinach are just a few highlights of the season, and all make excellent additions to your power bowls. They will boost your energy and health while satisfying your taste buds.

INGREDIENTS

Shaved Asparagus

1 bunch asparagus, ends trimmed

¼ cup thinly sliced red onion

¼ cup pine nuts

1 tablespoon extra-virgin olive oil

1 tablespoon freshly squeezed lemon juice

Pinch of sea salt

Pinch of freshly ground black pepper

For Serving

2 cups cooked pearl barley (page 196)

2 handfuls roughly chopped spinach

1 cup green peas

½ cup sliced radish

½ medium lemon, halved

½ cup Orange-Balsamic Vinaigrette (recipe follows)

Shaved Asparagus & Barley Bowl

with Orange-Balsamic Vinaigrette

Asparagus offers a number of health benefits and nutrients, including fiber, antioxidants, and vitamins. The best time to eat it is in early spring, when asparagus showcases its mild, earthy flavor. When buying, look for bright-green and firm stalks; for this recipe, thicker stalks are best for easier shaving with a peeler. Since asparagus doesn't store well, plan to use it within a day or two of purchase.

Makes 2 bowls

1. Prepare the asparagus salad. Shave each asparagus stalk with a sharp peeler to create thin, wide strands. In a medium bowl, combine the shaved asparagus, onion, pine nuts, oil, lemon juice, salt, and pepper, and toss well.

2. Assemble each bowl with half of the barley, asparagus salad, spinach, green peas, and radish. Garnish with a lemon wedge and drizzle with the vinaigrette.

Orange-Balsamic Vinaigrette

Makes about ½ cup

Juice from 1 small navel orange (about ¼ cup)

3 tablespoons extra-virgin olive oil

1 tablespoon balsamic vinegar

1 teaspoon pure maple syrup

Pinch of sea salt

Pinch of freshly ground black pepper

- In a small bowl, whisk together the orange juice, oil, vinegar, maple syrup, salt, and pepper. Taste and adjust the seasoning, if desired.

INGREDIENTS

Mushrooms & Peas

1 tablespoon avocado oil

¼ cup diced red onion

1 clove garlic, minced

2 cups sliced mushrooms, such as cremini, portobello, or shiitake

1 cup fresh or frozen green peas

1 teaspoon ground cumin

1 teaspoon ground sweet paprika

Dash of cayenne pepper

Cabbage Slaw

2 cups sliced red or green cabbage (or a combination of both)

1 cup julienned carrot

1 clove garlic, minced

1 tablespoon extra-virgin olive oil

1 tablespoon freshly squeezed lime juice

¼ teaspoon sea salt

For Serving

½ cup sliced radish

1 medium avocado, diced

1 tablespoon toasted sesame seeds

½ medium lemon, halved

½ cup Creamy Herb Dressing (recipe follows)

Pea, Mushroom & Cabbage Slaw Bowl with Creamy Herb Dressing

Green peas are a tasty spring staple, offering flavor, delicate sweetness, protein, and amino acids. While I always keep a bag of frozen peas on hand, as they do well in a pinch, I opt for fresh peas from the farmers' market when available. They combine well with most vegetables, but especially mushrooms, as in this bowl. The cabbage slaw serves as a crunchy counterpart to both of these tender ingredients.

Makes 2 bowls

1. Prepare the mushrooms and peas. In a medium skillet over low heat, warm the avocado oil. Add the onion and garlic and stir. Cook for a few minutes, until the garlic starts to become fragrant and the onion starts to become translucent. Increase the heat to medium and add the mushrooms, peas, cumin, paprika, and cayenne. Cook for about 10 minutes, or until the mushrooms are tender and the peas appear bright green. Turn off the heat.

2. Prepare the slaw. In a medium bowl, combine the cabbage, carrot, garlic, olive oil, lime juice, and salt. Mix well.

3. Assemble each bowl with half of the cabbage slaw, sautéed mushrooms and peas, radish, and avocado. Sprinkle with the sesame seeds, garnish with a lemon wedge, and serve with the dressing.

Creamy Herb Dressing

Makes about ½ cup

¼ cup raw cashews, soaked in water for 30 minutes
¼ cup water
¼ cup fresh cilantro leaves
¼ cup fresh parsley leaves
1 tablespoon fresh mint leaves
1 tablespoon extra-virgin olive oil
1 tablespoon freshly squeezed lemon juice
½ jalapeño pepper, seeded and sliced (optional)
1 clove garlic
Pinch of sea salt

- Rinse and drain the cashews. In a blender, combine the cashews, water, cilantro, parsley, mint, olive oil, lemon juice, jalapeño, garlic, and salt. Blend on high for 1 to 2 minutes, until smooth and creamy, scraping down the sides as needed. Taste and adjust the seasoning, if desired.

INGREDIENTS

2 cups cooked quinoa (page 194)
2 cups cooked chickpeas (page 192)
2 cups sugar snap peas, sliced
2 cups chopped romaine lettuce or spring mix
2 cups spinach, sliced
2 cups diced cucumber
½ cup diced carrot
½ cup diced radish
½ cup diced cherry tomato
1 medium avocado, diced
2 tablespoons thinly sliced green onion (green parts only)
2 tablespoons chopped fresh mint
½ cup Mustard Vinaigrette (recipe follows)
½ medium lemon, halved

Spring Chopped Salad Bowl
with Mustard Vinaigrette

Nothing says "spring" like a delicious chopped salad featuring peak-season radishes and sugar snap peas. Unlike most of the other bowls in this book, for this one I prefer to toss all of the ingredients like a salad to get a little of everything in each bite. The chickpeas and quinoa are optional but make a great source of added protein and fiber.

Makes 2 bowls

1. In a large bowl, combine the quinoa, chickpeas, sugar snap peas, lettuce, spinach, cucumber, carrot, radish, tomato, avocado, green onion, and mint. Stir well.

2. Divide between the two bowls and drizzle with the vinaigrette. Garnish each bowl with a lemon wedge.

Mustard Vinaigrette

Makes about ½ cup

⅓ cup extra-virgin olive oil
2 tablespoons balsamic vinegar
1 teaspoon Dijon mustard
1 clove garlic, minced
Pinch of sea salt
Pinch of freshly ground black pepper

- In a small bowl, whisk together the oil, vinegar, mustard, garlic, salt, and pepper. Taste and adjust the seasoning, if desired.

INGREDIENTS

Pickled Carrot & Cucumber

½ cup apple cider vinegar

2 tablespoons pure maple syrup

½ cup julienned carrot

½ cup thinly sliced cucumber

¼ teaspoon sea salt

For Serving

2 cups chopped green or red cabbage

1 cup chopped bok choy

1 cup julienned cucumber

½ cup fresh cilantro leaves

¼ cup chopped fresh mint

¼ cup chopped fresh basil

¼ cup thinly sliced green onion (green parts only)

¼ cup toasted peanuts or almonds, roughly chopped (optional)

1 jalapeño pepper, seeded and sliced

½ cup Sriracha-Lime Dressing (recipe follows)

½ medium lemon, halved

Vietnamese Banh Mi Bowl

with Sriracha-Lime Dressing

Banh mi is a Vietnamese term for bread or baguette that references a sandwich typically containing meat (most commonly pork), pickled cucumbers and carrots, sriracha, jalapeños, cilantro, mint, and mayonnaise. This bowl features the flavors of the original without the bread or meat. Crisp spring cabbage and bok choy are topped with pickled carrots, bright herbs, and a spicy dressing, making for a delicious spin on a classic.

Makes 2 bowls

1. Prepare the pickled carrot and cucumber. In a small pot, bring the vinegar and maple syrup to a bare simmer. Turn off the heat and add the carrot, thinly sliced cucumber, and salt. Stir occasionally while preparing the remaining ingredients.

2. Assemble each bowl with half of the cabbage, bok choy, julienned cucumber, cilantro, mint, basil, green onion, peanuts, and jalapeño. Top with the pickled carrot and cucumber and drizzle with the dressing. Garnish with a lemon wedge.

Sriracha-Lime Dressing

Makes about ½ cup

3 tablespoons freshly squeezed lime juice
2 tablespoons tamari
2 tablespoons water
1 tablespoon sriracha
1 tablespoon pure maple syrup
1 teaspoon minced peeled fresh ginger
1 clove garlic, minced
Pinch of sea salt
Pinch of freshly ground black pepper

- In a small bowl, whisk together the lime juice, tamari, water, sriracha, maple syrup, ginger, garlic, salt, and pepper. Taste and adjust the seasoning, if desired.

Vietnamese Banh Mi Bowl
(page 10)

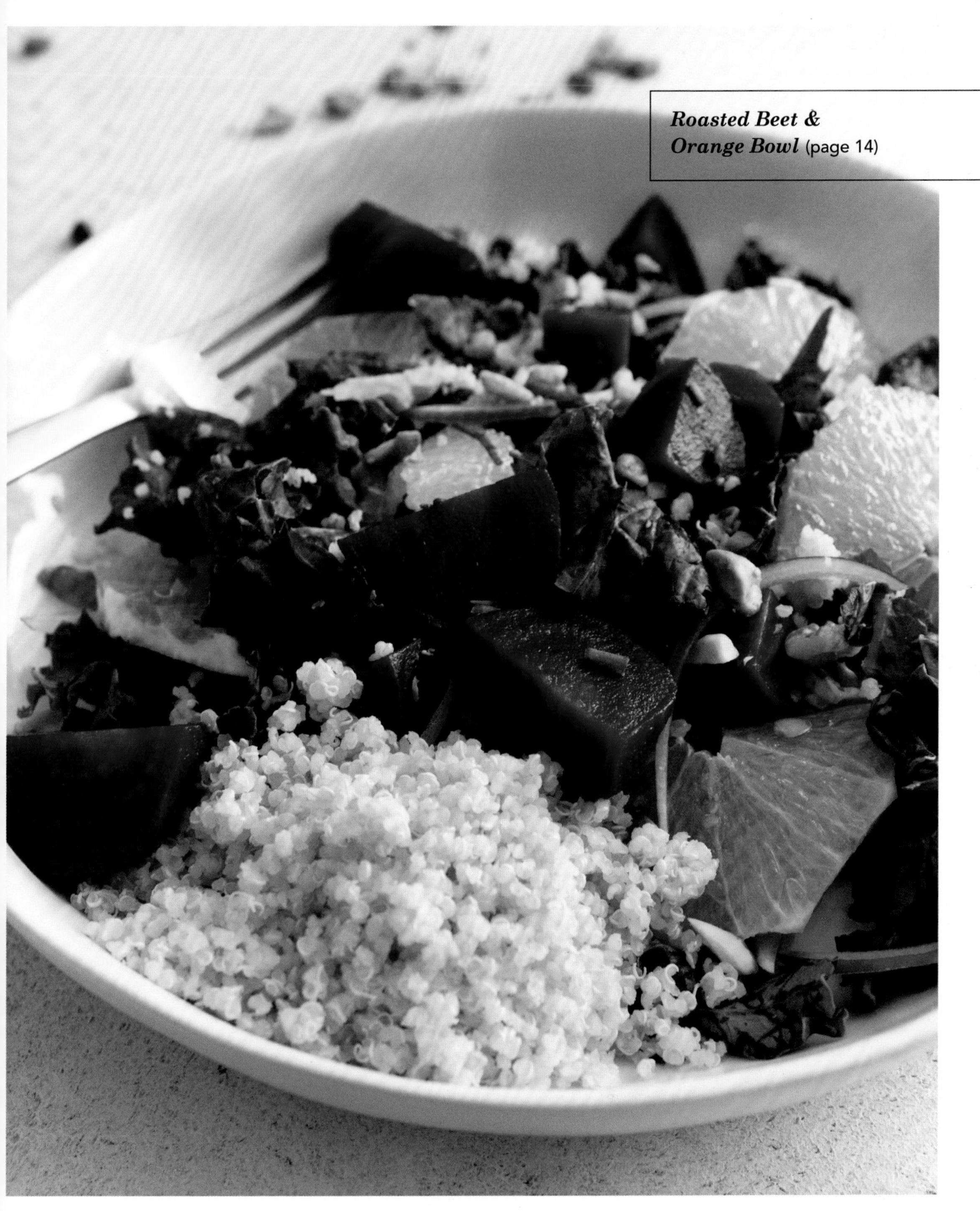

Roasted Beet & Orange Bowl (page 14)

INGREDIENTS

Roasted Beets

2 medium beets, peeled

1 tablespoon avocado oil

1 clove garlic, minced

Pinch of sea salt

1 tablespoon freshly squeezed lemon juice

Massaged Kale

2 cups stemmed and finely chopped kale

1 tablespoon extra-virgin olive oil

1 teaspoon freshly squeezed lemon juice

For Serving

2 cups cooked quinoa (page 194)

¼ cup chopped raw walnuts

¼ cup finely diced red onion

1 medium navel orange, peeled and sliced crosswise

2 tablespoons minced chives

2 tablespoons pepitas

¼ teaspoon sea salt

Pinch of freshly ground black pepper

½ cup Pistachio-Lemon Dressing (recipe follows)

Roasted Beet & Orange Bowl

with Pistachio-Lemon Dressing

Beets prefer cooler weather and make a great staple during the spring. They are a good source of vitamin C, fiber, and essential minerals. Seek out beets that are on the smaller side, with a firm texture, and store them in a bag in the coolest part of the fridge. This bowl features a medley of roasted beets, citrus, quinoa, and kale, and the pistachio dressing helps the flavors really pop. It tastes as delicious as it looks.

Makes 2 bowls

1. Prepare the beets. Preheat the oven to 400 degrees F. Slice each beet into quarters (if any of the quarters are bigger than an inch, slice them one more time). In a medium bowl, toss the beets with the avocado oil,

garlic, and salt. Wrap the beets in aluminum foil and place them on a baking sheet. Roast for 30 to 45 minutes, until the beets are tender (stick a toothpick or fork into them to make sure). Remove from the oven and drizzle with the lemon juice. Taste and adjust the seasoning, if desired.

2. Prepare the kale. Massage the kale with the olive oil and lemon juice for a couple minutes by hand, until it's tender and shiny.

3. Assemble each bowl with half of the quinoa, roasted beets, kale, walnuts, onion, navel orange, chives, pepitas, salt, and pepper. Serve with the dressing.

> ***Note***
>
> If you're short on time, many grocery stores stock precooked beets that can be used as an alternative to roasting your own.

Pistachio-Lemon Dressing

Makes about ½ cup

¼ cup raw pistachios, soaked in water for 30 minutes
¼ cup extra-virgin olive oil
2 tablespoons freshly squeezed lemon juice
2 tablespoons hemp seeds
1 clove garlic
Pinch of sea salt
Pinch of freshly ground black pepper

- In a blender, combine the pistachios, oil, lemon juice, hemp seeds, garlic, salt, and pepper. Blend on high for about 1 minute, until smooth and creamy, scraping down the sides as needed. Taste and adjust the seasoning, if desired.

INGREDIENTS

Masala Chickpeas

1 tablespoon avocado oil

1 clove garlic, minced

2 cups cooked chickpeas (page 192)

3 tablespoons water (or more for a curry consistency)

1 teaspoon ground sweet paprika

½ teaspoon chili powder

½ teaspoon ground cumin

¼ teaspoon ground turmeric

¼ teaspoon garam masala (optional)

¼ teaspoon sea salt

¼ teaspoon freshly ground black pepper

For Serving

2 cups cooked rice (page 195)

1 cup diced cucumber

1 cup diced radish

1 cup cherry tomatoes, halved

¼ cup thinly sliced green onion (green parts only)

½ cup Cilantro Chutney (recipe follows)

½ medium lemon, halved

Masala Chickpea Buddha Bowl

with Cilantro Chutney

Indian food was the first type of food I ever learned how to cook, thanks to my mother, and chickpeas (or *chole*) were one of my favorite dishes as a child. In Hindi, the word *masala* refers to a mixture of spices. This bowl uses turmeric, cumin, and garam masala, which are traditional to many Indian dishes. The cilantro chutney is simple but pairs especially well with the chickpeas and vegetables here.

Makes 2 bowls

Continued on next page

1. Prepare the chickpeas. In a medium saucepan over low heat, warm the oil and garlic. After a few minutes, add the chickpeas, water, paprika, chili powder, cumin, turmeric, garam masala, salt, and pepper. Mix well and increase the heat to medium. Cook for about 10 minutes, or until the chickpeas start to turn golden brown. Taste and adjust the seasoning, if desired. Turn off the heat.

2. Assemble each bowl with half of the rice, chickpeas, cucumber, radish, tomatoes, and green onion. Serve with the chutney and garnish with a lemon wedge.

Cilantro Chutney

Makes about ½ cup

1 cup fresh cilantro leaves
¼ cup water
1 tablespoon freshly squeezed lime juice
1 teaspoon minced green chili pepper (optional)
½ teaspoon minced peeled fresh ginger
¼ teaspoon ground cumin
Pinch of sea salt
Pinch of freshly ground black pepper

- In a blender, combine the cilantro, water, lime juice, green chili, ginger, cumin, salt, and pepper. Blend on high for about 1 minute, until smooth and creamy, scraping down the sides as needed. Taste and adjust the seasoning, if desired.

INGREDIENTS

Cilantro-Lime Cauliflower Rice

1 tablespoon avocado oil

2 cups cauliflower rice (page 191) or cooked brown or white rice (page 195)

¼ cup finely chopped fresh cilantro

Pinch of sea salt

1 tablespoon freshly squeezed lime juice

Black Beans

2 cups cooked black beans (page 192)

¼ cup finely diced red onion

1 red Fresno chili pepper, halved crosswise and thinly sliced (optional)

½ teaspoon ground cumin

¼ teaspoon sea salt

¼ teaspoon freshly ground black pepper

For Serving

2 handfuls spinach (about 2 cups), roughly chopped

½ cup sliced radish

¼ cup fresh cilantro leaves

2 tablespoons thinly sliced green onion (green parts only)

½ medium lemon, halved

½ cup Creamy Herb Dressing (page 7)

Black Bean & Cilantro-Lime Cauliflower Rice Bowl

with Creamy Herb Dressing

This Mexican-inspired bowl is packed with flavor and nutrition while still hitting all the comfort buttons. The cauliflower rice has a hint of lime flavor, and the creamy dressing is reminiscent of garden-fresh herbs with a touch of heat from the pepper. This bowl makes for an easy-to-transport weekday lunch—reheating optional.

Makes 2 bowls

Continued on next page

1. Prepare the cauliflower rice. In a medium skillet over medium-low heat, warm the oil. Add the cauliflower rice, cilantro, and salt. Cook for about 10 minutes, stirring frequently, until the cauliflower rice is slightly cooked through. Turn off the heat, drizzle with the lime juice, and stir.
2. Prepare the beans. In a medium bowl, combine the beans, onion, chili pepper, cumin, salt, and black pepper. Mix well. Taste and adjust the seasoning, if desired.
3. Assemble each bowl with half of the spinach, cauliflower rice, black beans, radish, cilantro, and green onion. Garnish with a lemon wedge and drizzle with the dressing.

INGREDIENTS

Polenta

4 cups water

½ teaspoon sea salt

1 cup polenta

1 tablespoon avocado oil

Mushrooms

1 tablespoon avocado oil

2 cups chopped mushrooms, such as cremini, portobello, or shiitake

Pinch of sea salt

Pinch of freshly ground black pepper

For Serving

2½ cups thinly sliced spinach

½ cup diced tomato

2 tablespoons diced red onion

½ cup Walnut-Kale Pesto (recipe follows)

½ medium lemon, halved

Soft Polenta & Mushroom Bowl

with Walnut-Kale Pesto

In this bowl the strong flavor of pesto is paired with savory sautéed mushrooms and warm creamy polenta, which is simple to prepare. Traditionally, pesto is made with basil and pine nuts. However, this variation uses kale and walnuts to make a highly nutritious and flavorful pesto sauce. The addition of fresh tomatoes, spinach, and onion add fiber and make for a hearty, satisfying meal and create a beautiful presentation.

Makes 2 bowls

1. Prepare the polenta. In a medium pot, bring the water to a boil. Add the salt. Slowly pour in the polenta while stirring. Add the avocado oil,

reduce the heat to low, and cover. Cook for about 30 minutes, stirring occasionally, until the polenta is soft.

2. Prepare the mushrooms. In a small skillet over medium heat, warm the oil. Add the mushrooms, salt, and pepper. Cook for 5 minutes, stirring frequently. Turn off the heat.
3. Assemble each bowl with half of the polenta, mushrooms, spinach, tomato, and onion. Top with a dollop of pesto and garnish with a lemon wedge.

Walnut-Kale Pesto

Makes about ½ cup

2 tablespoons raw walnuts, soaked in water for 30 minutes
¼ cup stemmed and roughly chopped kale
¼ cup extra-virgin olive oil
2 tablespoons water
1 teaspoon freshly squeezed lemon juice
1 clove garlic
Pinch of sea salt
Pinch of freshly ground black pepper

- Rinse and drain the walnuts. In a blender or food processor, combine the walnuts, kale, oil, water, lemon juice, garlic, salt, and pepper. Blend on high for about 2 minutes, until smooth and creamy, scraping down the sides as needed. Taste and adjust the seasoning, if desired.

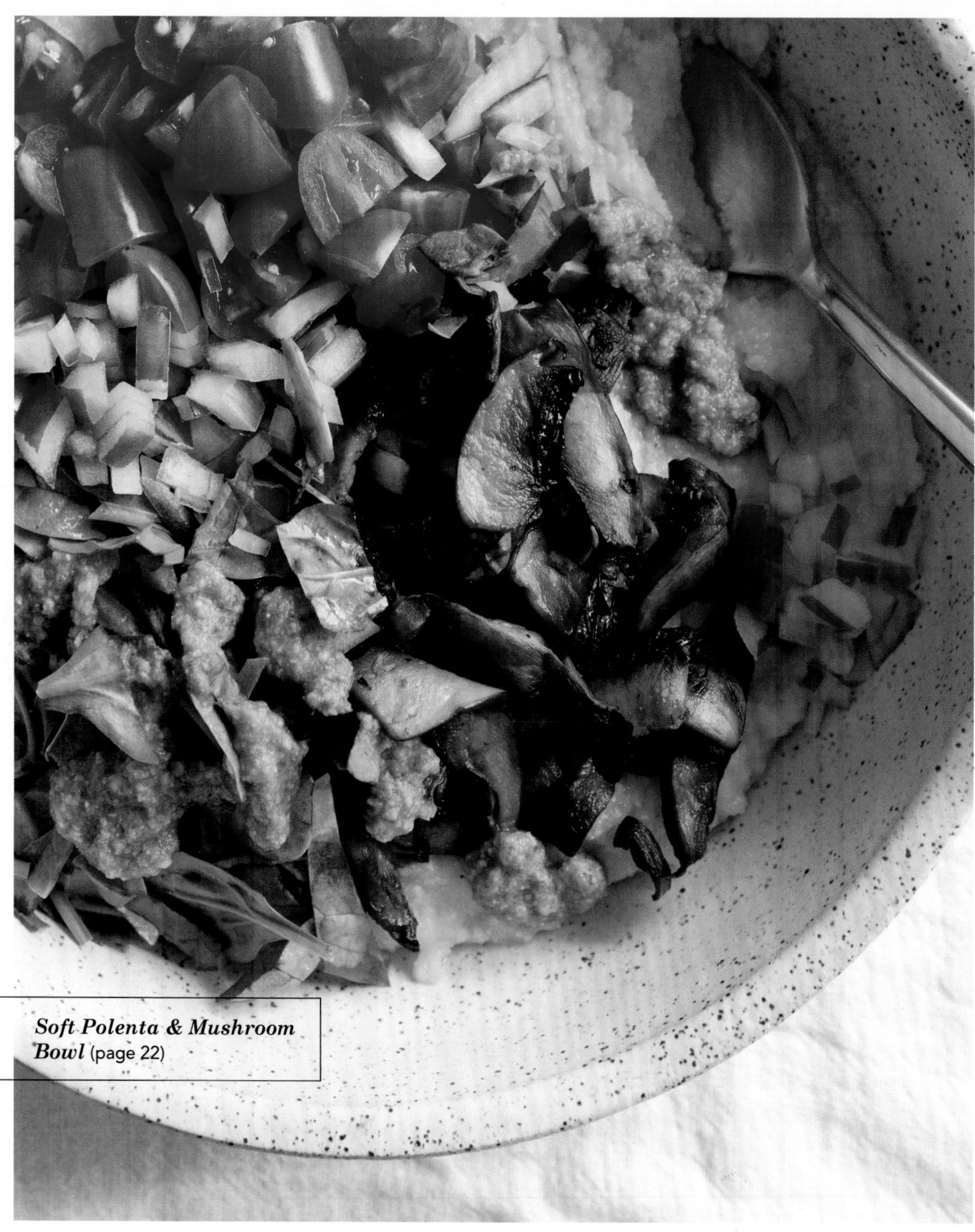

Soft Polenta & Mushroom Bowl (page 22)

Thai Veggie Rice Bowl
(page 26)

INGREDIENTS

Cauliflower–Green Pea Rice

2 cups cauliflower rice (page 191) or cooked brown or white rice (page 195)

2 cups green peas

1 tablespoon avocado oil

¼ teaspoon sea salt

¼ cup fresh cilantro, finely chopped

For Serving

2 cups spinach

1 red bell pepper, chopped

1 cup shredded red cabbage

1 cup julienned carrot

1 cup bean sprouts

1 cup thinly sliced radish

¼ cup thinly sliced green onion (green parts only)

¼ cup toasted almonds or peanuts, roughly chopped

½ cup Spicy Nut Dressing (recipe follows)

½ medium lemon, halved

Thai Veggie Rice Bowl
with Spicy Nut Dressing

This bowl is truly powered by plants. With eight different vegetables, it makes for a refreshing and filling meal. What's more, it's adaptable: many simple modifications can be made in the name of variety or personal preference. White or brown rice can be swapped for the cauliflower rice, edamame or fava beans for the green peas, chard or kale for the spinach, and parsley for the cilantro. What's indisputable is how well the spicy nut dressing brings it all together.

Makes 2 bowls

1. Prepare the rice. In a medium skillet over medium heat, combine the cauliflower rice, peas, oil, salt, and cilantro. Cook for 10 minutes, stirring frequently, until the rice and green peas are tender. Turn off the heat.

2. Assemble each bowl with half of the cauliflower–green pea rice, spinach, pepper, cabbage, carrots, sprouts, radish, and green onion. Top with the nuts and drizzle with the dressing. Garnish with a lemon wedge.

Spicy Nut Dressing

Makes about ½ cup

¼ cup peanut or almond butter (page 188)
¼ cup water
1 tablespoon extra-virgin olive oil
1 tablespoon freshly squeezed lime juice
1 tablespoon tamari
1½ teaspoons pure maple syrup
½ teaspoon grated peeled fresh ginger
Pinch of sea salt
Pinch of cayenne pepper

- In a blender, combine the peanut butter, water, oil, lime juice, tamari, maple syrup, ginger, salt, and cayenne. Blend on high for about 1 minute, until smooth and creamy, scraping down the sides as needed. Taste and adjust the seasoning, if desired.

INGREDIENTS

Pickled Radish & Onion

½ cup thinly sliced radish

½ cup thinly sliced red onion

½ cup apple cider vinegar

¼ teaspoon sea salt

½ teaspoon pure maple syrup

Black Beans

1 tablespoon avocado oil

2 cups cooked black beans (page 192)

¼ cup finely diced red onion

1 clove garlic, minced

½ teaspoon ground cumin

½ teaspoon ground sweet paprika

¼ teaspoon sea salt

¼ teaspoon freshly ground black pepper

Dash of cayenne pepper

For Serving

2 cups cooked quinoa (page 194)

1 cup grated parsnip

1 medium avocado, sliced

1 cup roughly chopped fresh cilantro

½ medium lime, halved

½ cup Avocado-Herb Dressing (recipe follows)

Black Bean & Parsnip Taco Bowl
with Avocado-Herb Dressing

This Mexican-inspired bowl packs an energy punch with its healthy fats and protein, making it an excellent choice for lunch or dinner. The parsnip and pickled radish and onion add crunch and a nice sour note. The dressing is reminiscent of sour cream in texture and can alternatively be used as a dip by halving the amount of water.

Makes 2 bowls

Continued on next page

1. Prepare the radish and onion. In a small bowl, combine the radish, onion, vinegar, salt, and maple syrup. Let sit for 30 minutes while you prepare the remaining ingredients.
2. Prepare the beans. In a medium skillet over medium heat, warm the oil. Add the black beans, onion, garlic, cumin, paprika, salt, black pepper, and cayenne. Cook for about 5 minutes, stirring occasionally, until the onions are fragrant and the beans are warmed through. Turn off the heat.
3. Assemble each bowl with half of the quinoa, black beans, parsnip, avocado, cilantro, and pickled radish and onion. Garnish with a lime wedge and serve with the dressing.

Avocado-Herb Dressing

Makes about ½ cup

¼ medium avocado
¼ cup unsweetened almond milk or water
¼ cup chopped fresh cilantro
2 tablespoons extra-virgin olive oil
1 tablespoon freshly squeezed lime juice
Pinch of sea salt
Pinch of freshly ground black pepper

- In a blender, combine the avocado, almond milk, cilantro, oil, lime juice, salt, and pepper. Blend on high for 1 to 2 minutes, until smooth and creamy, scraping down the sides as needed. Taste and adjust the seasoning, if desired.

INGREDIENTS

Spring Vegetable Mix

1 tablespoon avocado oil

1 clove garlic, minced

2 cups shelled and peeled fava beans

1 bunch asparagus, ends trimmed

¼ teaspoon sea salt

¼ teaspoon freshly ground black pepper

1 tablespoon freshly squeezed lemon juice

Crispy Shallots

1 tablespoon avocado oil

1 shallot, thinly sliced

Pinch of sea salt

For Serving

2 cups spinach, roughly chopped

2 cups cooked quinoa (page 194)

1 cup sliced strawberries

½ cup sliced radish

½ medium lemon, halved

½ cup Mustard Vinaigrette (page 9)

Fava Bean & Asparagus Bowl

with Mustard Vinaigrette

This bowl combines the freshest flavors of spring with asparagus and fava beans. The crispy shallots add a little crunchiness, while the strawberries balance the savory with a touch of sweetness. This bowl not only pleases the taste buds, but also leaves you feeling energized, making it a perfect candidate for lunch to help you push past the afternoon slump.

Makes 2 bowls

Continued on next page

1. Prepare the vegetable mix. In a medium skillet over low heat, warm the oil. Add the garlic and cook for a few minutes, stirring frequently. Increase the heat to medium and add the fava beans, asparagus, salt, and pepper. Cook for about 10 minutes, or until the asparagus is bright and tender. Turn off the heat and drizzle with the lemon juice.

2. Prepare the crispy shallots. In a small skillet over medium heat, warm the oil. Add the shallots and salt. Cook, stirring occasionally, until the shallots are crispy and golden brown, about 10 minutes. Turn off the heat.

3. Assemble each bowl with half of the spinach, quinoa, vegetable mix, strawberries, radish, and crispy shallots. Garnish with a lemon wedge and drizzle with the vinaigrette.

INGREDIENTS

Tandoori Chickpeas

2 cups cooked chickpeas (page 192)
1 tablespoon freshly squeezed lemon juice
1 tablespoon avocado oil
1 clove garlic, minced
1 teaspoon minced peeled fresh ginger
1 teaspoon ground sweet paprika
½ teaspoon ground cumin
½ teaspoon ground turmeric
½ teaspoon ground coriander (optional)
¼ teaspoon sea salt
¼ teaspoon freshly ground black pepper
Dash of cayenne pepper

For Serving

2 cups roughly chopped spinach
1 cup cherry tomatoes, halved
¼ cup diced red onion
½ cup fresh cilantro leaves
½ medium lemon, halved
½ cup Creamy Mint Chutney (recipe follows)

Tandoori Chickpea & Spinach Bowl

with Creamy Mint Chutney

A tandoori is a type of cylindrical clay oven commonly used in India that can reach temperatures of 900 degrees F. This bowl recreates the essence of this traditional cooking method with a blend of flavorful Indian spices. The chickpeas are roasted to provide crispy texture, and my spin on the mint chutney uses cashews to add a layer of creaminess.

Makes 2 bowls

1. Prepare the chickpeas. Preheat the oven to 425 degrees F and line a baking sheet with parchment paper. In a medium bowl, combine the

chickpeas, lemon juice, oil, garlic, ginger, paprika, cumin, turmeric, coriander, salt, black pepper, and cayenne. Toss well and spread the chickpeas in a single layer on the baking sheet. Bake for 20 to 25 minutes, stirring a few times, until the chickpeas are golden brown.

2. Assemble each bowl with half of the chickpeas, spinach, tomatoes, onion, and cilantro. Garnish with a lemon wedge and serve with the chutney.

Creamy Mint Chutney

Makes about ½ cup

¼ cup raw cashews, soaked in water for 30 minutes
½ cup chopped fresh mint
½ cup chopped fresh cilantro
3 tablespoons water, plus more as needed
2 tablespoons diced yellow onion
1 tablespoon freshly squeezed lemon juice
1 teaspoon minced seeded green chili pepper (optional)
1 clove garlic, minced
½ teaspoon minced peeled fresh ginger
¼ teaspoon ground cumin
¼ teaspoon sea salt
Pinch of freshly ground black pepper

- Rinse and drain the cashews. In a blender, combine the cashews, mint, cilantro, water, onion, lemon juice, chili pepper, garlic, ginger, cumin, salt, and black pepper. Blend on high for about 1 minute, until smooth and creamy, scraping down the sides as needed. Add more water, if needed. Taste and adjust the seasoning, if desired.

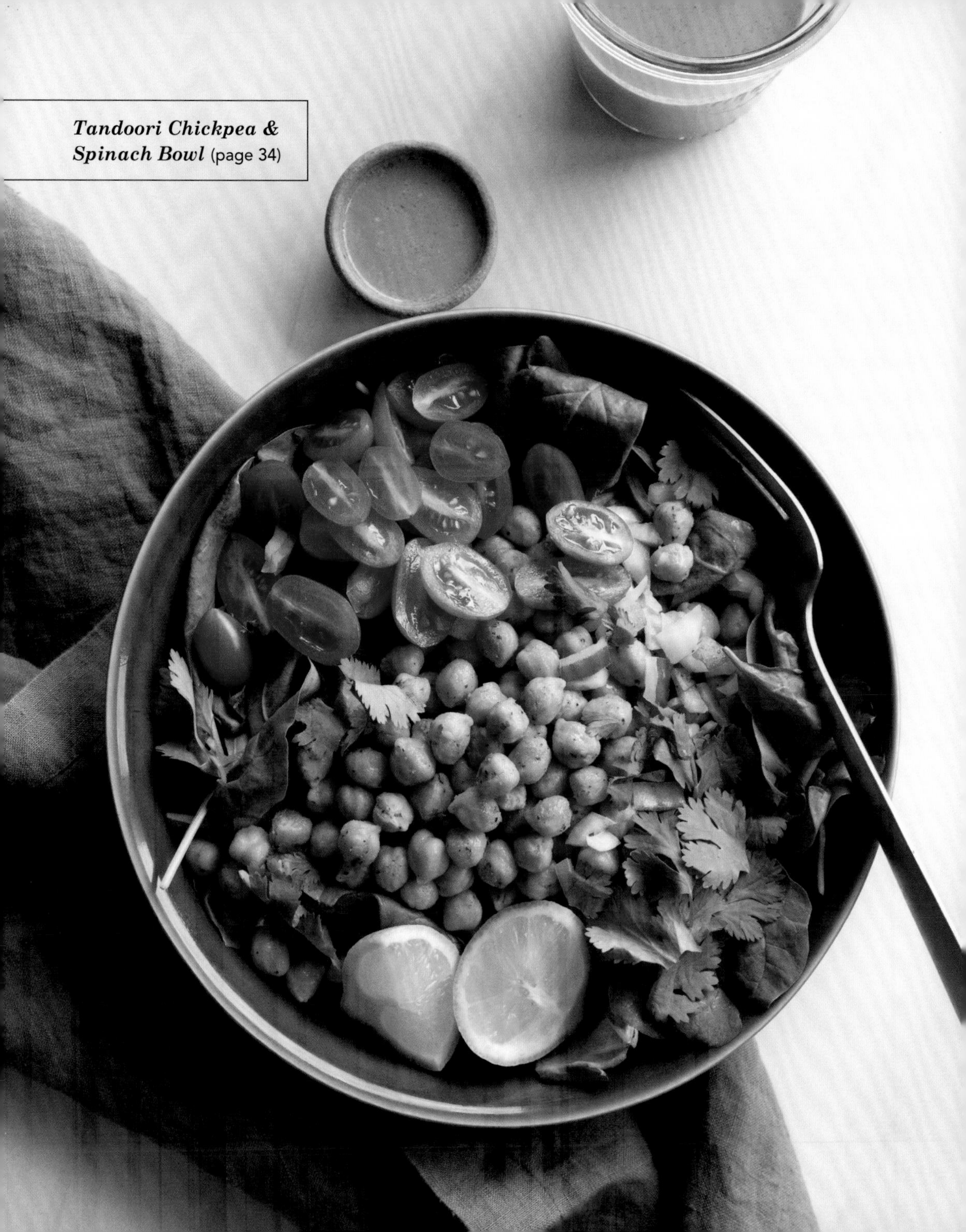

Tandoori Chickpea & Spinach Bowl (page 34)

Fennel & Lentil Bowl
(page 38)

INGREDIENTS

Fennel & Lentils

1 tablespoon avocado oil

2 cups cooked lentils (page 193)

½ cup finely diced fennel bulb

½ teaspoon ground cumin

½ teaspoon ground turmeric

½ teaspoon ground sweet paprika

¼ teaspoon sea salt

¼ teaspoon freshly ground black pepper

1 tablespoon freshly squeezed lemon juice

For Serving

2 cups spinach, roughly chopped

1 cup cooked millet (page 196)

1 cup diced cucumber

½ cup sliced radish

½ medium lemon, halved

½ cup Turmeric-Ginger Vinaigrette (recipe follows)

Fennel & Lentil Bowl

with Turmeric-Ginger Vinaigrette

Lentils are versatile, tasty, and easy to prepare, and since they aren't too heavy, they make a perfect candidate for spring eating. They are commonly used in Indian and French dishes and offer a delicious source of protein. The turmeric dressing enhances this warming but light bowl, though you can omit it altogether if desired.

Makes 2 bowls

1. Prepare the lentils. In a medium pot over medium heat, combine the oil, lentils, fennel, cumin, turmeric, paprika, salt, and pepper. Cook, stirring, for 10 minutes, or until the fennel is cooked through. Turn off the heat and drizzle with the lemon juice. Taste and adjust the seasoning, if desired.

2. Assemble each bowl with half of the spinach, millet, fennel and lentils, cucumber, and radish. Garnish with a lemon wedge and drizzle with the dressing.

Turmeric-Ginger Vinaigrette

Makes about ½ cup

¼ cup extra-virgin olive oil

2 tablespoons freshly squeezed lemon juice

1 teaspoon ground turmeric

1 teaspoon finely minced peeled fresh ginger

Pinch of sea salt

- In a small bowl, whisk together the oil, lemon juice, turmeric, ginger, and salt. Alternatively, combine the ingredients in a blender and blend on high for 1 minute until smooth and creamy, scraping down the sides as needed. Taste and adjust the seasoning, if desired.

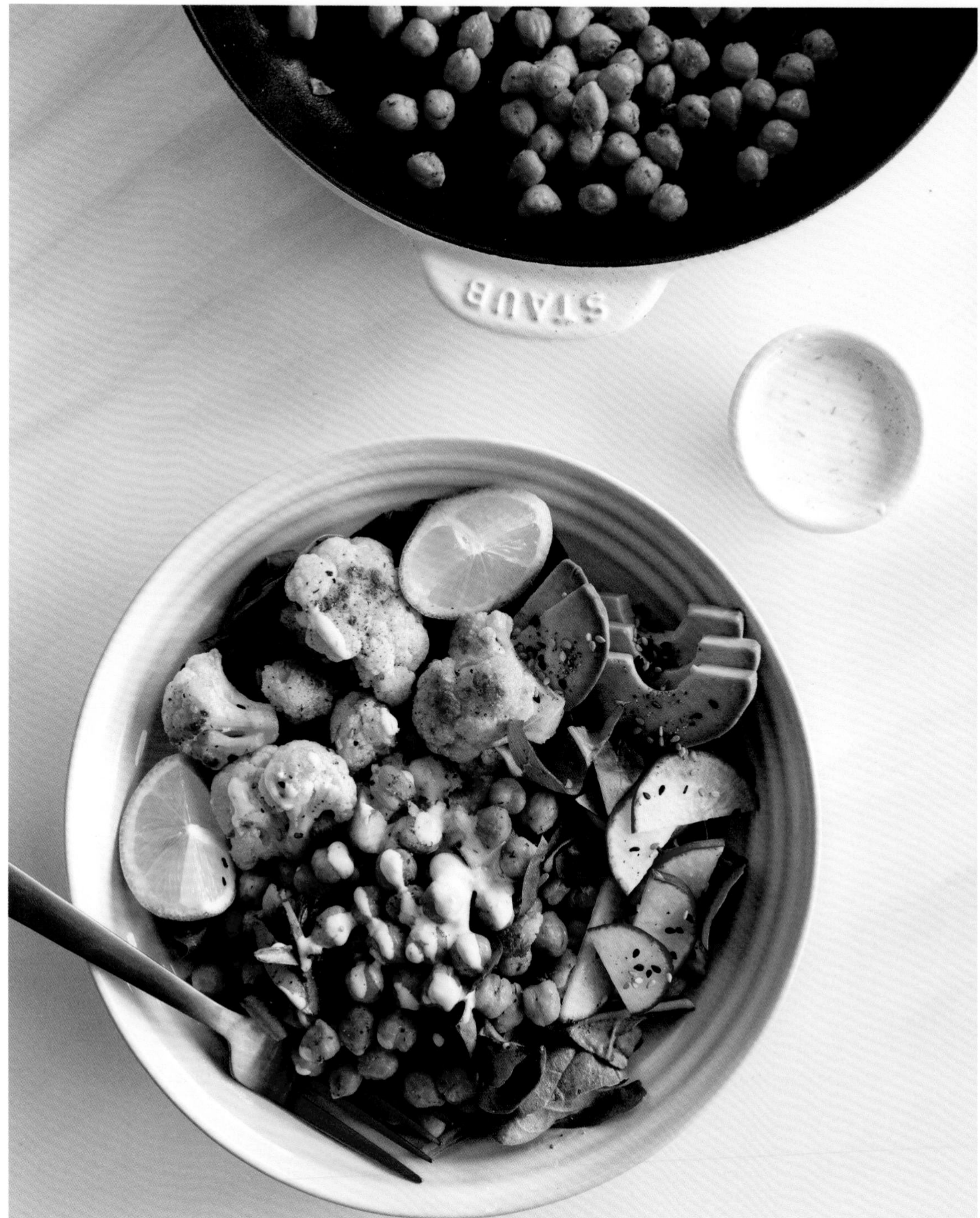
STAUB

INGREDIENTS

Turmeric Cauliflower

3 cups bite-size cauliflower florets

1 tablespoon avocado oil

1 tablespoon freshly squeezed lemon juice

1 clove garlic, minced

¼ teaspoon ground turmeric

¼ teaspoon sea salt

¼ teaspoon freshly ground black pepper

Garlicky Chickpeas

1 tablespoon avocado oil

2 cups cooked chickpeas (page 192)

1 clove garlic, minced

¼ teaspoon sea salt

¼ teaspoon freshly ground black pepper

For Serving

2 cups spinach, roughly chopped

½ cup sliced radish

1 medium avocado, sliced

1 teaspoon toasted sesame seeds

½ cup Cucumber-Dill Dressing (recipe follows)

½ medium lemon, halved

Roasted Turmeric Cauliflower & Garlicky Chickpea Bowl

with Cucumber-Dill Dressing

Yellow turmeric, green spinach, and red radishes make this bowl vibrantly colorful. The garlicky chickpeas add flavor, while the spinach and radish bring the nutrition and crunch of spring. This bowl can be made ahead of time, so it's perfect for on-the-go meals.

Makes 2 bowls

1. Prepare the cauliflower. Preheat the oven to 450 degrees F and line a baking sheet with parchment paper. In a medium mixing bowl, combine

Continued on next page

the cauliflower, oil, lemon juice, garlic, turmeric, salt, and pepper. Toss the florets until they are evenly coated. Spread on the baking sheet in a single layer and roast for 15 minutes, flipping them halfway through. Remove from the oven and set aside.

> ***Note***
>
> Turmeric easily stains everything it touches, so handle with care!

2. Prepare the chickpeas. In a medium skillet over medium heat, warm the oil. Add the chickpeas, garlic, salt, and pepper. Stir to coat the chickpeas. Cook for 10 to 15 minutes, stirring frequently, until the chickpeas are fragrant and golden brown. Turn off the heat.

3. Assemble each bowl with half of the spinach, roasted cauliflower, chickpeas, radish, avocado, and sesame seeds. Drizzle with the dressing and garnish with a lemon wedge.

Cucumber-Dill Dressing

Makes about ½ cup

¼ cup raw cashews, soaked in water for 30 minutes
¼ cup water
¼ cup chopped cucumber
1½ tablespoons freshly squeezed lemon juice
1 tablespoon extra-virgin olive oil
1½ teaspoons minced fresh dill
1 clove garlic
Pinch of sea salt

- Rinse and drain the cashews. In a blender, combine the cashews, water, cucumber, lemon juice, oil, dill, garlic, and salt. Blend on high for about 1 minute, until smooth and creamy, scraping down the sides as needed. Taste and adjust the seasoning, if desired.

INGREDIENTS

Falafel

2 cups cooked brown lentils (page 193) or chickpeas (page 192)

2 tablespoons avocado oil, plus more for frying

¼ cup diced yellow onion

¼ cup raw walnuts

¼ cup chopped fresh parsley

1 teaspoon ground cumin

1 teaspoon ground coriander (optional)

¼ teaspoon ground turmeric

¼ teaspoon cayenne pepper

¼ teaspoon sea salt

¼ teaspoon freshly ground black pepper

For Serving

2 handfuls roughly chopped romaine lettuce

1 cup kalamata olives, halved

1 cup diced cucumber

1 cup cherry tomatoes, halved

1 cup hummus (page 190)

¼ cup finely diced red onion

¼ cup finely chopped fresh cilantro

½ cup Cashew Tzatziki (recipe follows)

Mediterranean Lentil "Falafel" Bowl

with Cashew Tzatziki

I had my first bite of Mediterranean food in my early twenties. "Where has this been all my life?" I remember thinking while eating that falafel sandwich. This bowl is a nod to that first taste, combining Indian and Mediterranean herbs and spices to make lentil falafel—a little different from the traditional ones made with chickpeas. The falafel are then served on a bed of crisp raw vegetables, olives, and hummus for a savory and nutritious bowl.

Makes 2 bowls

Continued on next page

1. Prepare the falafel. In a food processor, combine the lentils, oil, yellow onion, walnuts, parsley, cumin, coriander, turmeric, cayenne, salt, and black pepper. Process until the ingredients are combined and crumbly, 2 to 3 minutes. Form into 1½-inch balls. In a large skillet over medium heat, warm the oil. Cook the falafel in batches, without crowding them, for 5 minutes per side, until golden brown.

2. Assemble each bowl with half of the lettuce, olives, cucumber, tomatoes, hummus, red onion, and cilantro. Add the falafel and drizzle with the tzatziki.

Cashew Tzatziki

Makes about ½ cup

¼ cup raw cashews, soaked in water for 30 minutes
¼ cup diced cucumber
¼ cup water
2 tablespoons freshly squeezed lemon juice
1 tablespoon tahini
1 teaspoon minced fresh dill
1 clove garlic, minced
¼ teaspoon sea salt

- Rinse and drain the cashews. In a blender or food processor, combine the cashews, cucumber, water, lemon juice, tahini, dill, garlic, and salt. Blend on high for about 1 minute, until smooth and creamy, scraping down the sides as needed. Taste and adjust the seasoning, if desired.

Summer Bowls

Summer Garden Patch Bowl
(page 52)

As the temperatures start to rise, I look to incorporate more raw, bright ingredients into my meals. This includes using ripe, juicy fruits in my smoothies and bowls—or eating them on their own (hello, watermelon!)—but also loading up on all the vegetables summer has to offer. From arugula to zucchini, there's so much to love and enjoy. It also tastes better, since produce that was just harvested and hasn't traveled far is fresher and contains more nutrients.

When I first started on my health journey, I didn't know what it meant to eat "in season." Since all varieties of fresh produce are easily accessible throughout North America year-round, I would frequently find myself buying strawberries and blueberries in winter or brussels sprouts and pomegranates in summer. As my understanding progressed, I became more aware of how eating seasonally benefited my health, the quality of my food, and the impact on my wallet.

Summer is one of the easiest times to buy seasonal, local produce, which can reduce your carbon footprint and help your local economy. I encourage you to spend time at your neighborhood farmers' market to better understand where your food comes from and meet the hardworking farmers behind it. This has been one of the most transformational pieces of my relationship with food—see what it can do for you.

INGREDIENTS

Fried Cauliflower Rice

2 tablespoons avocado oil

1 clove garlic, minced

½ teaspoon minced peeled fresh ginger

2 cups cauliflower rice (page 191) or cooked brown or white rice (page 195)

1 cup fresh or frozen green peas

½ cup diced carrot

½ cup diced red bell pepper

½ cup sliced cremini mushrooms

1 cup diced fresh or frozen pineapple

2 tablespoons tamari

1 teaspoon chili powder

¼ teaspoon sea salt

¼ teaspoon freshly ground black pepper

¼ cup sliced green onion (green parts only)

For Serving

¼ cup fresh basil leaves, thinly sliced

¼ cup raw cashews, roughly chopped

2 tablespoons kimchi (optional)

Sriracha (optional)

Pineapple Fried Cauliflower Rice Bowl

The star of this bowl is the pineapple, which peaks in late spring and into early summer and adds a subtle sweetness to an otherwise savory compilation of vegetables, including mushrooms and peppers. Unlike traditional fried rice, this bowl uses cauliflower rice. Because it reheats well, I tend to make twice the amount I need so I can enjoy another meal of it during the week.

Makes 2 bowls

1. Prepare the cauliflower rice. In a medium skillet over low heat, warm the oil. Once warm, add the garlic and ginger, stirring occasionally, until they start to brown slightly, about 2 minutes. Add the cauliflower rice, green peas, carrot, bell pepper, and mushrooms. Stir until the ingredients are well coated in oil.

2. Cook for 3 to 5 minutes, until the cauliflower has softened slightly. Drizzle in the tamari and add the pineapple. Increase the heat to medium-high and stir well. Add the chili powder, salt, black pepper, and green onion. Cook for 5 more minutes, stirring well, until the vegetables are tender and cooked through. Turn off the heat.
3. Assemble each bowl with half of the fried rice, basil, cashews, and kimchi. Drizzle with sriracha.

INGREDIENTS

1 small zucchini
2 cups cooked tricolor quinoa (page 194)
2 cups arugula
1 cup cherry tomatoes, halved
1 cup fresh corn kernels
1 cup diced cucumber
¼ cup thinly sliced red onion
¼ cup pitted kalamata olives
2 tablespoons pepitas
2 tablespoons toasted sesame seeds (optional)
1 medium avocado, sliced
½ medium lemon, halved
½ cup Creamy Basil Pesto (recipe follows)

Summer Garden Patch Bowl

with Creamy Basil Pesto

This bowl brings together the vegetables you'd find growing in a summer garden, thus the name. It's not overly complicated, but it's certainly not lacking in beauty or flavor. This energy-boosting bowl is ideal for a day at either the beach or the office and can be made ahead of time.

Makes 2 bowls

1. Shave the zucchini lengthwise with a vegetable peeler (you should have 1 cup of ribbons).
2. Assemble each bowl with half of the zucchini ribbons, quinoa, arugula, tomatoes, corn, cucumber, onion, olives, pepitas, sesame seeds, and avocado.
3. Garnish with a lemon wedge and serve with the pesto.

Creamy Basil Pesto

Makes about ½ cup

1 cup fresh basil leaves

½ avocado

¼ cup raw pine nuts

3 tablespoons extra-virgin olive oil

1 tablespoon water

1 tablespoon freshly squeezed lemon juice

Pinch of sea salt

Pinch of freshly ground black pepper

- In a food processor, combine the basil, avocado, pine nuts, olive oil, water, lemon juice, salt, and pepper. Pulse for about 2 minutes, until smooth and creamy, scraping down the sides as needed. Taste and adjust the seasoning, if desired.

INGREDIENTS

1 cup cooked brown or white rice (page 195)
1 cup shelled edamame
1 cup chopped cucumber
1 cup chopped nori strips (optional)
1 medium avocado, sliced
½ cup shredded or julienned carrot
½ cup shredded or thinly sliced red cabbage
½ cup diced fresh mango
2 tablespoons sliced green onion (green parts only)
1 tablespoon toasted sesame seeds
½ cup Spicy Sriracha Dressing (recipe follows)
½ medium lime, halved

Deconstructed Sushi Bowl

with Spicy Sriracha Dressing

This bowl is made from all the ingredients commonly used to make plant-based sushi, but it doesn't require any nori-rolling skills. It contains fresh mango for a delicate, sweet flavor; cucumber, carrots, and cabbage for crunch; avocado for creamy, healthy fat; and a spicy dressing for balanced heat. If you'd like to incorporate even more vegetables, replace the white or brown rice with cauliflower rice.

Makes 2 bowls

1. Assemble each bowl with half of the rice, edamame, cucumber, nori strips, avocado, carrot, cabbage, mango, and green onion. Sprinkle with the sesame seeds.
2. Drizzle with the dressing and serve with a lime wedge.

Spicy Sriracha Dressing

Makes about ½ cup

¼ cup raw cashews, soaked in water for 30 minutes

¼ cup water

1 tablespoon freshly squeezed lemon juice

1 tablespoon sriracha

1 tablespoon tamari

1 tablespoon toasted sesame oil

Pinch of sea salt

Pinch of freshly ground black pepper

- Rinse and drain the cashews. In a blender, combine the cashews, water, lemon juice, sriracha, tamari, sesame oil, salt, and pepper. Blend on high for 1 to 2 minutes, until smooth and creamy, scraping down the sides as needed. Taste and adjust the seasoning, if desired.

INGREDIENTS

2 big handfuls arugula
2 cups cooked chickpeas (page 192)
2 cups cooked quinoa (page 194)
2 cups diced watermelon (about 1-inch cubes)
½ cup blueberries
2 tablespoons fresh mint leaves
2 tablespoons pepitas
½ medium lime, halved
½ cup Creamy Cashew Dressing (recipe follows)

Watermelon & Arugula Bowl

with Creamy Cashew Dressing

This bowl is perfect for a day at the beach or the park because it's light and hydrating and packs well. The watermelon, blueberries, chickpeas, quinoa, and fresh greens combine to make a sweet and savory summer staple dish. If you do plan to take this dish along on an adventure, be sure to store the creamy dressing separately to prevent the ingredients from getting soggy.

Makes 2 bowls

1. Assemble each bowl with half of the arugula, chickpeas, quinoa, watermelon, blueberries, mint, and pepitas.
2. Garnish with a lime wedge and drizzle with the dressing.

Creamy Cashew Dressing

Makes about ½ cup

½ cup raw cashews, soaked in water for 30 minutes

½ cup water

2 tablespoons freshly squeezed lemon juice

2 tablespoons extra-virgin olive oil

Pinch of sea salt

Pinch of freshly ground black pepper

- Rinse and drain the cashews. In a blender, combine the cashews, water, lemon juice, oil, salt, and pepper. Blend on high for about 1 minute, until smooth and creamy, scraping down the sides as needed. Taste and adjust the seasoning, if desired.

INGREDIENTS

Zucchini Salad

1 large zucchini

¼ cup pepitas

1 tablespoon freshly squeezed lemon juice

1 tablespoon extra-virgin olive oil

Pinch of sea salt

Pinch of freshly ground black pepper

For Serving

2 cups cooked chickpeas (page 192)

¼ cup dry-packed sun-dried tomatoes

¼ cup fresh basil leaves, roughly chopped

½ cup Walnut-Kale Pesto (page 23)

Zucchini Noodle Bowl

with Walnut-Kale Pesto

One of my favorite ways to enjoy fresh zucchini at the height of summer is by turning it into noodles. With the help of a spiralizer or vegetable peeler, it becomes a delicious substitute for traditional pasta. The zucchini can be eaten raw, but if you prefer it cooked, simply sauté it in a little oil—just be sure to thoroughly dry the noodles or ribbons beforehand. If you don't have sun-dried tomatoes, substitute halved cherry tomatoes instead.

Makes 2 bowls

1. Prepare the zucchini salad. Shave the zucchini lengthwise with a vegetable peeler or spiralize it using a spiralizer. In a medium bowl, toss the zucchini noodles with the pepitas, lemon juice, oil, salt, and pepper.

2. Assemble each bowl with half of the zucchini noodles, chickpeas, and sun-dried tomatoes. Garnish with the basil and drizzle with the pesto.

INGREDIENTS

Tabbouleh

2 cups finely minced stemmed kale

2 cups cooked quinoa (page 194)

2 cups cooked chickpeas (page 192)

1 cup finely diced cucumber

½ cup cherry tomatoes, quartered

¼ cup finely minced fresh parsley

¼ cup finely diced celery

¼ cup finely diced red onion

1 tablespoon freshly squeezed lemon juice

1 tablespoon avocado oil

2 sprigs mint, leaves finely minced

½ teaspoon sea salt

¼ teaspoon freshly ground black pepper

For Serving

½ cup kalamata olives, halved

½ cup Hummus Dressing (recipe follows)

½ medium lemon, halved

Quinoa Tabbouleh Bowl

with Hummus Dressing

Tabbouleh is a vegetarian salad with Lebanese roots that is traditionally made with finely chopped tomatoes, onion, parsley, and mint. It's usually served as a side dish, but to make it a meal, this bowl features chickpeas, kale, and kalamata olives for added substance. The hummus dressing that tops it all off is one of my go-to favorites; it's also fantastic drizzled over a simple salad.

Makes 2 bowls

1. Prepare the tabbouleh. In a large bowl, combine the kale, quinoa, chickpeas, cucumber, tomatoes, parsley, celery, onion, lemon juice, oil, mint, salt, and pepper. Mix well. Taste and adjust the seasoning, if desired.

2. Assemble each bowl with half of the tabbouleh and olives. Drizzle with the dressing and garnish with a lemon wedge.

Hummus Dressing

Makes about ½ cup

¼ cup hummus (page 190)

¼ cup water

1 tablespoon freshly squeezed lemon juice

¼ teaspoon ground cumin

Pinch of sea salt

Pinch of freshly ground black pepper

- In a blender, combine the hummus, water, lemon juice, cumin, salt, and pepper. Blend on high for about 1 minute, until smooth and creamy, scraping down the sides as needed. Taste and adjust the seasoning, if desired.

INGREDIENTS

1 cup shelled edamame
1 cup sliced green cabbage
1 cup sliced red cabbage
1 cup diced cucumber
1 cup bean sprouts
1 red bell pepper, thinly sliced
1 medium avocado, diced
½ cup julienned carrot
½ cup chopped fresh cilantro
¼ cup sliced green onion (green parts only)
¼ cup raw cashews, roughly chopped
½ cup Cilantro-Lime Dressing (recipe follows)

Fresh Thai Summer Bowl

with Cilantro-Lime Dressing

This refreshing raw bowl is packed with crunch, thanks to the green and red cabbages, red bell pepper, and cucumber. Though the dish has no grain and minimal protein—you could add either, if desired—it's substantial and filling. The cilantro-lime dressing is light and flavorful with just a touch of heat. If you want to add more texture as well as visual appeal, use a peeler or mandoline to create ribbons with the cucumber instead of dicing it.

Makes 2 bowls

1. Assemble each bowl with half of the edamame, green and red cabbage, cucumber, bean sprouts, bell pepper, avocado, carrot, cilantro, green onion, and cashews.
2. Drizzle with the dressing.

Cilantro-Lime Dressing

Makes about ½ cup

½ cup roughly chopped fresh cilantro
¼ cup extra-virgin olive oil
¼ cup water
1 tablespoon freshly squeezed lime juice
½ jalapeño pepper, seeded and diced (optional)
1 clove garlic, minced
Pinch of sea salt
Pinch of freshly ground black pepper

- In a blender, combine the cilantro, oil, water, lime juice, jalapeño, garlic, salt, and black pepper. Blend on high for about 1 minute, until smooth and creamy, scraping down the sides as needed. Taste and adjust the seasoning, if desired.

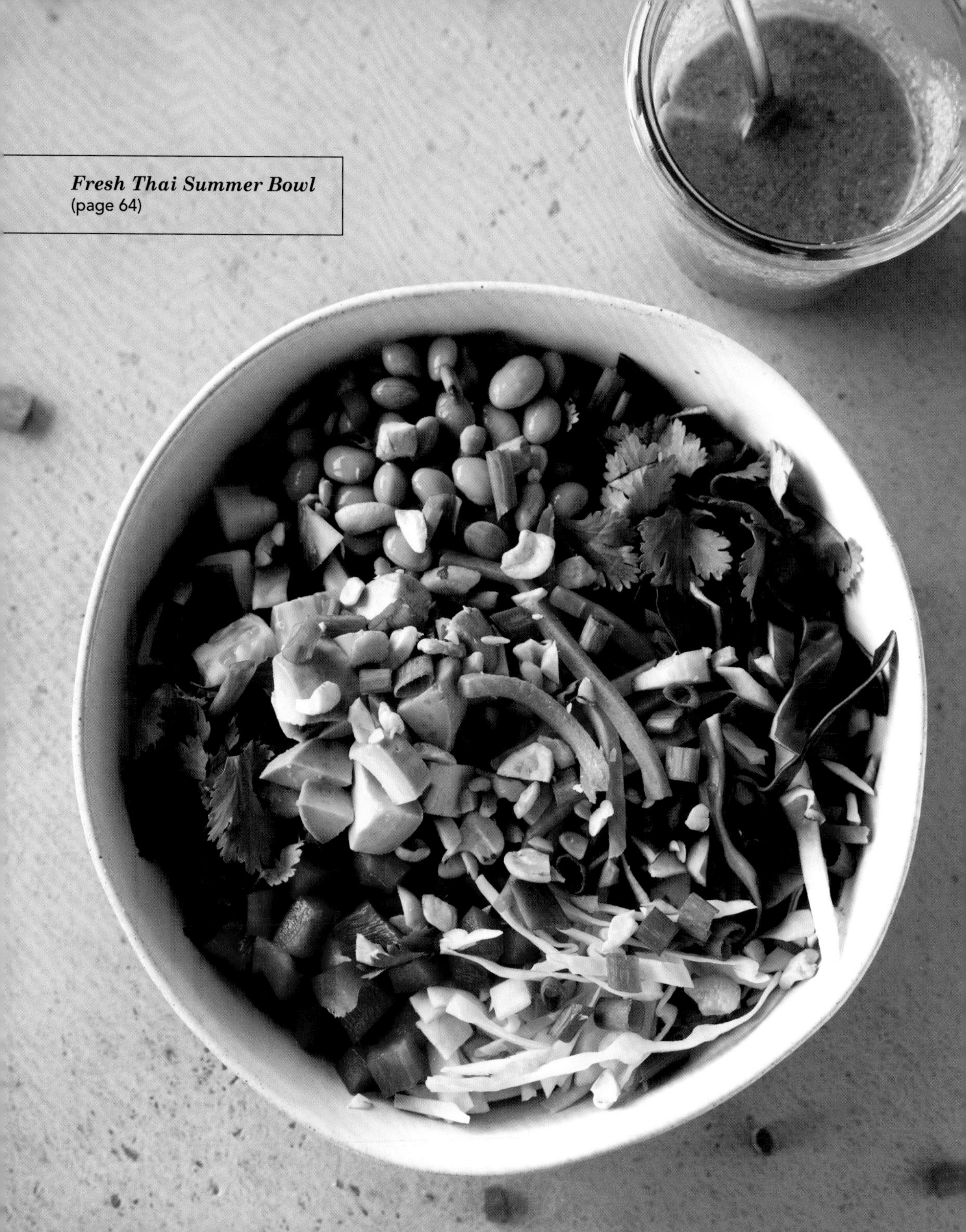

Fresh Thai Summer Bowl
(page 64)

Mexican Veggie Fajita Bowl (page 68)

INGREDIENTS

Fajitas

1 green bell pepper, sliced

1 red bell pepper, sliced

1 red onion, sliced

1 medium zucchini, cut into half-moons

2 tablespoons avocado oil

1 tablespoon freshly squeezed lemon juice

1 clove garlic, grated, or ¼ teaspoon garlic powder

1 teaspoon ground sweet paprika

½ teaspoon ground cumin

¼ teaspoon sea salt

¼ teaspoon freshly ground black pepper

Chickpeas

1 tablespoon avocado oil

2 cups cooked chickpeas (page 192)

1 teaspoon chili powder

½ teaspoon garlic powder

½ teaspoon ground cumin

¼ teaspoon sea salt

¼ teaspoon freshly ground black pepper

1 teaspoon freshly squeezed lime juice

For Serving

½ cup chopped fresh cilantro

1 cup tortilla chips (optional)

1 medium avocado, sliced

½ medium lime, halved

¾ cup Cilantro-Lime Salsa (recipe follows)

Mexican Veggie Fajita Bowl

with Cilantro-Lime Salsa

This plant-based version of fajitas skips the usual meat, but you won't miss it. The cilantro-lime salsa is so delicious you might be tempted to finish it off even without a basket of chips nearby. If you want something a little more authentic, feel free to replace the chickpeas with pinto or black beans.

Makes 2 bowls

1. Prepare the vegetables. In a container with a lid, combine the green and red bell peppers, onion, and zucchini. In a small bowl, whisk together the oil, lemon juice, garlic, paprika, cumin, salt, and pepper. Pour the marinade over the vegetables and stir until well coated. Cover and set aside for at least 45 minutes.
2. Prepare the chickpeas. In a medium skillet over medium heat, warm the oil. Add the chickpeas, chili powder, garlic powder, cumin, salt, and pepper. Cook for 5 to 7 minutes, stirring occasionally, until the chickpeas are soft. Turn off the heat, drizzle with lime juice, and stir well.
3. In a medium skillet over high heat, add the marinated vegetables. Stir occasionally until the vegetables are lightly charred, 3 to 5 minutes.
4. Assemble each bowl with half of the chickpeas, fajitas, cilantro, tortilla chips, and avocado. Garnish with a lime wedge and serve with the salsa.

Cilantro-Lime Salsa

Makes about ¾ cup

½ cup diced tomato
¼ cup minced fresh cilantro
2 tablespoons diced red onion
2 tablespoons diced seeded jalapeño pepper
1 tablespoon freshly squeezed lime juice
1 tablespoon extra-virgin olive oil
1 clove garlic, minced
½ teaspoon ground cumin
Pinch of sea salt
Pinch of freshly ground black pepper

- In a small bowl, combine the tomato, cilantro, onion, jalapeño, lime juice, oil, garlic, cumin, salt, and pepper and mix well. Cover and set aside in the refrigerator until ready to serve. Taste and adjust the seasoning, if desired.

INGREDIENTS

1 cup roughly chopped spinach
1 cup roughly chopped radicchio
½ medium navel orange, peeled and sliced
½ medium grapefruit, peeled and sliced
2 cups shelled edamame
1 medium avocado, sliced
¼ cup thinly sliced red onion
Pinch of sea salt
Pinch of freshly ground black pepper
¼ cup pepitas
¼ cup toasted hazelnuts, roughly chopped
2 tablespoons chopped fresh mint
½ cup Lemon-Tahini Dressing (recipe follows)

Summer Citrus Bowl
with Lemon-Tahini Dressing

In this bowl, slices of heart-healthy avocado are paired with fresh citrus, spinach, and radicchio for a delicate combination that's just as stunning to view as it is to eat. The pepitas and hazelnuts offer a pleasantly crunchy counterpart to the tender fruits and vegetables, and the mint adds a refreshing note. This dish is a perfect candidate for a day at the beach—just be sure to slice the avocado right before you're ready to enjoy the bowl, so it doesn't start to brown.

Makes 2 bowls

1. Assemble each bowl with half of the spinach, radicchio, orange, grapefruit, edamame, avocado, onion, salt, and pepper.
2. Top with pepitas, hazelnuts, and mint. Serve with the dressing.

Lemon-Tahini Dressing

Makes about ½ cup

¼ cup water

2 tablespoons tahini

2 tablespoons freshly squeezed lemon juice

2 tablespoons extra-virgin olive oil

1 clove garlic, minced

½ teaspoon ground cumin

Pinch of sea salt

- In a small bowl, whisk together the water, tahini, lemon juice, oil, garlic, cumin, and salt until smooth and creamy. Alternatively, combine the ingredients in a blender and blend on high for 1 minute, scraping down the sides as needed. Taste and adjust the seasoning, if desired.

INGREDIENTS

2 cups thinly sliced spinach
2 cups cooked quinoa (page 194)
2 cups cooked chickpeas (page 192)
1 cup thinly sliced radicchio
1 cup hummus (page 190)
½ cup cherry tomatoes, halved
¼ cup roughly chopped fresh cilantro
¼ cup diced red onion
¼ cup pitted kalamata olives
½ jalapeño pepper, seeded and thinly sliced
½ medium lime, halved
½ cup Cucumber-Dill Dressing (page 42)

Mediterranean Buddha Bowl

with Cucumber-Dill Dressing

This recipe offers a classic, everyday bowl bursting with flavor, fresh ingredients, and nutrition. It is made with chickpeas, quinoa, and plenty of vegetables and is drizzled with a cooling cucumber-dill dressing. If the quinoa and chickpeas are prepared in advance, this bowl takes but a few minutes to pull together.

Makes 2 bowls

1. Assemble each bowl with half of the spinach, quinoa, chickpeas, radicchio, hummus, tomatoes, cilantro, onion, olives, and jalapeño.
2. Garnish with a lime wedge and serve with the dressing or drizzle it on top.

INGREDIENTS

Spiced Chickpeas

1½ cups cooked chickpeas (page 192)

1 tablespoon avocado oil

1 teaspoon ground sweet paprika

½ teaspoon ground cumin

½ teaspoon ground ginger

½ teaspoon ground turmeric

¼ teaspoon sea salt

¼ teaspoon freshly ground black pepper

Dash of cayenne pepper

For Serving

2 medium Yukon Gold potatoes (about 10 ounces)

1 cup diced tomato

1 cup diced cucumber

½ cup roughly chopped fresh cilantro

¼ cup diced red onion

½ teaspoon sea salt

½ cup Creamy Mint Chutney (page 35)

½ medium lemon, halved

Indian Chaat Bowl

with Creamy Mint Chutney

When I was younger, my family and I would travel to India every few summers. One of my favorite memories was eating street food, especially the flavorful, spicy potatoes seasoned with Indian spices and herbs. *Chaat* is a Hindi word that typically refers to any savory snack served from food stalls and carts. While *chaat* is usually composed of deep-fried ingredients, this bowl is a healthier version inspired by the traditional Indian snack, with roasted chickpeas, crisp vegetables, and bright herbs.

Makes 2 bowls

1. Prepare the chickpeas. Preheat the oven to 375 degrees F. Line a baking sheet with parchment paper. In a medium bowl, combine the chickpeas, oil, paprika, cumin, ginger, turmeric, salt, black pepper, and cayenne.

Toss to coat the chickpeas. Spread in a single layer on the baking sheet and bake for 25 minutes, shaking the pan a few times, until they are golden. Remove from the oven and set aside to cool down.

2. Meanwhile, bring a medium pot of water to a boil. Add the potatoes and boil for 20 minutes, or until soft. Carefully remove the potatoes and let them cool down. Peel off the skins and cut each potato into small cubes.

3. Assemble each bowl with half of the potatoes, chickpeas, tomato, cucumber, cilantro, onion, and salt. Drizzle with the chutney and garnish with a lemon wedge.

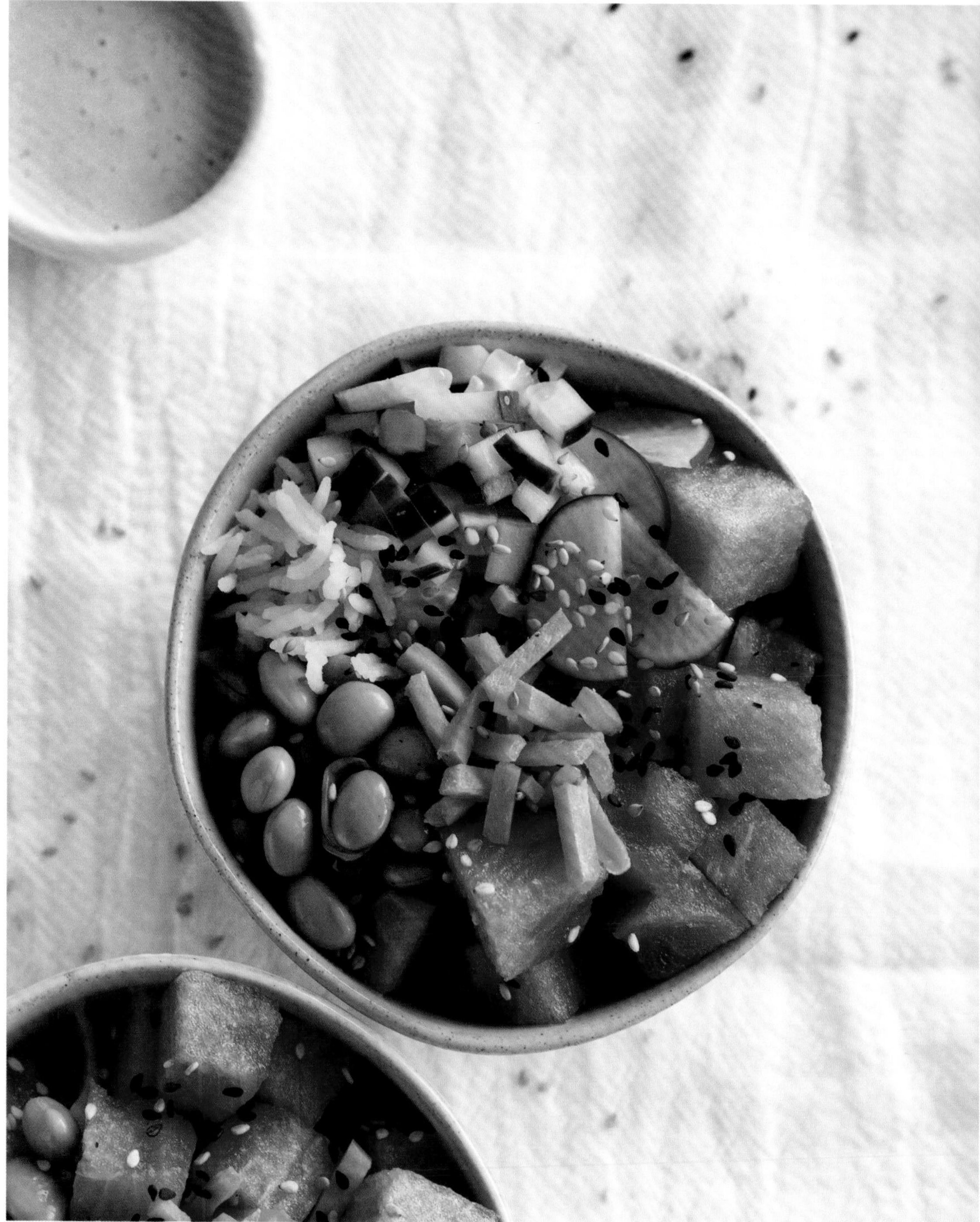

INGREDIENTS

2 cups cooked brown or white rice (page 195)
3 cups diced watermelon
1 cup shelled edamame
½ cup sliced radish
½ cup julienned carrot
½ cup diced cucumber
¼ cup finely diced red onion
1 medium avocado, diced
2 tablespoons toasted sesame seeds
½ cup Spicy Sriracha Dressing (page 56)

Watermelon Poke Bowl
with Spicy Sriracha Dressing

Poke is a raw-fish salad in Hawaiian cuisine. When poke bowls started popping up in restaurants everywhere, I felt a little left out because, while I don't eat fish, I admire how beautiful these bowls look. I decided I would celebrate a juicy summertime staple by making my own poke bowl featuring watermelon as a substitute for the fish. Here is my simple yet satisfying take, which will cool and refresh on a hot day.

Makes 2 bowls

1. Assemble each bowl with half of the rice, watermelon, edamame, radish, carrot, cucumber, onion, and avocado.
2. Sprinkle with toasted sesame seeds and drizzle with the dressing.

INGREDIENTS

Quinoa

1½ cups water

1 cup uncooked quinoa, rinsed and drained

½ cup full-fat coconut milk

¼ teaspoon sea salt

Mango Salsa

1 mango, diced

1 jalapeño pepper, seeded and finely minced

¼ cup chopped fresh cilantro

2 tablespoons thinly sliced green onion (green parts only)

1 tablespoon freshly squeezed lime juice

Pinch of sea salt

Pinch of freshly ground black pepper

For Serving

2 cups cooked black beans (page 192)

½ cup chopped red bell pepper

1 medium avocado, sliced

½ cup raw almonds, roughly chopped

½ cup Coconut-Cashew Dressing (recipe follows)

Island Black Bean–Quinoa Bowl

with Mango Salsa & Coconut-Cashew Dressing

This recipe may look like it has a little too much going on, but I promise every part contributes to a greater sum. The mango salsa is a particular highlight, offsetting the bowl's savory flavors with a delicate sweetness. The quinoa is cooked in a little coconut milk for a tropical, summery flair.

Makes 2 bowls

1. Prepare the quinoa. In a small pot, combine the water, quinoa, coconut milk, and salt. Bring to a boil, reduce to a simmer, and cover. Cook for 15 to 20 minutes, until the liquid is absorbed.

Continued on next page

2. Prepare the mango salsa. In a medium bowl, combine the mango, jalapeño, cilantro, green onion, lime juice, salt, and pepper. Mix well.

3. Assemble each bowl with half of the quinoa, black beans, bell pepper, avocado, almonds, and mango salsa. Drizzle with the dressing.

Coconut-Cashew Dressing

Makes about ½ cup

½ cup full-fat coconut milk

2 tablespoons raw cashews, soaked in water for 30 minutes

1 tablespoon freshly squeezed lemon juice

Pinch of sea salt

- In a blender, combine the coconut milk, cashews, lemon juice, and salt. Blend on high for about 1 minute, until smooth and creamy, scraping down the sides as needed. Taste and adjust the seasoning, if desired.

INGREDIENTS

1 tablespoon avocado oil
¼ cup diced yellow onion
1 cup uncooked white rice
1 cup green beans, cut into 1-inch pieces
½ cup cherry tomatoes, halved
½ cup diced carrot
1 teaspoon ground sweet paprika
½ teaspoon chili powder
½ teaspoon ground turmeric
½ teaspoon ground cumin
½ teaspoon sea salt
½ teaspoon freshly ground black pepper
¼ teaspoon ground coriander
Pinch of cayenne pepper (optional)
2 cups water
1 cup cooked chickpeas (page 192)
½ cup Creamy Turmeric Dressing (recipe follows)

Vegetable Pilaf Bowl
with Creamy Turmeric Dressing

Pilaf is the term used for rice cooked in seasoned broth. The rice is typically sautéed in oil before the spices and broth are added. The vegetables in this bowl give the pilaf texture, nutrients, and flavor. This is a great potluck dish, as it tastes delicious both warm and at room temperature. The creamy turmeric dressing is reminiscent of a yogurt-based sauce my mother would always make with her pilaf when I was growing up.

Makes 2 bowls

1. Prepare the pilaf. In a medium pot over low heat, warm the oil. Add the onion and cook for about 5 minutes, stirring occasionally, until it starts to become translucent. Increase the heat to medium and add the rice.

Continued on next page

Cook for 3 minutes, stirring frequently, until the rice starts to brown slightly. Add the beans, tomatoes, carrot, paprika, chili powder, turmeric, cumin, salt, black pepper, coriander, and cayenne.

2. Add the water and bring to a boil. Reduce the heat to a simmer, cover, and cook the pilaf for 20 minutes, until the water is mostly absorbed and the rice is soft. Add the chickpeas and cook for 10 additional minutes, until the water is completely absorbed. Gently mix. Taste and adjust the seasoning, if desired.

3. Assemble each bowl with half of the pilaf and serve with the dressing.

Creamy Turmeric Dressing

Makes about ½ cup

¼ cup raw cashews, soaked in water for 30 minutes
¼ cup water
½ teaspoon ground turmeric
½ teaspoon ground cumin
2 tablespoons freshly squeezed lemon juice
1 clove garlic, minced
Pinch of cayenne pepper
Pinch of sea salt

- Rinse and drain the cashews. In a blender, combine the cashews, water, turmeric, cumin, lemon juice, garlic, cayenne, and salt. Blend on high for about 1 minute, until smooth and creamy, scraping down the sides as needed. Taste and adjust the seasoning, if desired.

INGREDIENTS

Strawberry-Spinach Mix

2 cups roughly chopped spinach

2 cups cooked farro (page 197)

2 cups cooked chickpeas (page 192)

1 cup thinly sliced strawberries

1 tablespoon extra-virgin olive oil

¼ teaspoon sea salt

¼ teaspoon freshly ground black pepper

For Serving

½ cup roughly chopped toasted pecans

½ medium lemon, halved

½ cup Almond-Ginger Dressing (recipe follows)

Strawberry Spinach Bowl

with Toasted Pecans & Almond-Ginger Dressing

This recipe takes the traditional strawberry and spinach salad and turns it into a nourishing bowl with farro and chickpeas. It's light, a little sweet, and savory. The toasted pecans add crunch, healthy fat, and flavor. The almond-ginger dressing is one of my favorites, as it pairs well with the strawberries. This is a staple summer bowl.

Makes 2 bowls

1. Prepare the strawberry-spinach mix. In a large bowl, combine the spinach, farro, chickpeas, strawberries, oil, salt, and pepper. Stir gently to evenly coat the mixture with the oil. Taste and adjust the seasoning, if desired.

2. Assemble each bowl with half of the strawberry-spinach mix and toasted pecans. Garnish with a lemon wedge and serve with the dressing.

Almond-Ginger Dressing

Makes about ½ cup

¼ cup almond butter (page 188)

¼ cup water

2 tablespoons freshly squeezed lemon juice

1 teaspoon pure maple syrup

½ teaspoon grated peeled fresh ginger

Pinch of sea salt

- In a blender, combine the almond butter, water, lemon juice, maple syrup, ginger, and salt. Blend on high for about 1 minute, until smooth and creamy, scraping down the sides as needed. Taste and adjust the seasoning, if desired.

Fall Bowls

White Bean & Crispy Rosemary Potato Bowl (page 90)

The autumn harvest brings with it hearty and healthy produce, like pumpkins, brussels sprouts, apples, butternut squash, sweet potatoes, beets, carrots, and parsnips. The crisp, cool weather invites us to warm up by roasting them all to revel in the earthy flavors and toothsome, caramelized textures.

Fall is a great season to spend more time in the kitchen, trying out new recipes and reframing our idea of what constitutes comfort food. It's an opportunity to nourish our bodies and souls with self-care and to move inward as we head into the cooler months.

A simple self-care practice can be developed by following a set daily routine. Perhaps you've tried this before but struggled; reflect on why you've been unable to maintain it. Try simplifying your activities and then slowly adding more as you get into a self-care rhythm and start experiencing its power. Check in with yourself on a weekly basis and make adjustments as needed; I schedule this time for myself every Sunday.

Another goal might be to clear your kitchen space as the holidays approach. This could include stocking your pantry with cool-climate staples. Clear out any cans and packages that no longer serve your specific health needs, passing them along to a food bank or someone else in need. Let go of what's no longer serving you to make space for the new year to come.

INGREDIENTS

Rosemary Potatoes

3 medium Yukon Gold potatoes (about 1 pound), peeled

1 tablespoon minced fresh rosemary, or 1 teaspoon dried

1 tablespoon avocado oil

Pinch of sea salt

Pinch of freshly ground black pepper

Bean Mixture

2 cups cooked cannellini beans (page 192)

¼ cup diced red onion

¼ cup fresh cilantro leaves

1 tablespoon extra-virgin olive oil

1 tablespoon freshly squeezed lemon juice

1 clove garlic, minced

¼ teaspoon sea salt

¼ teaspoon freshly ground black pepper

Kale & Apple Salad

2 cups stemmed and roughly chopped kale

1 tablespoon extra-virgin olive oil

1 medium carrot, shaved into ribbons using a peeler or mandoline (about 1 cup)

½ cup diced apple

½ cup pepitas

1 teaspoon freshly squeezed lemon juice

Pinch of sea salt

Pinch of freshly ground black pepper

For Serving

1 medium avocado, sliced

½ medium lemon, halved

½ cup Cashew-Cumin Dressing (recipe follows)

White Bean & Crispy Rosemary Potato Bowl with Cashew-Cumin Dressing

Pairing beans with fresh fall vegetables like potatoes, kale, and carrots gives you a taste of the season while still filling you up. The cumin dressing was inspired by the spiced dish I ate growing up, *aloo sabzi*, which is a simple Indian preparation of potatoes cooked in cumin and other spices. You can opt for another source of protein instead of the cannellini beans, such as black or pinto beans.

Makes 2 bowls

1. Prepare the potatoes. Preheat the oven to 425 degrees F. Slice each potato into wedges by cutting it in half lengthwise, and then cutting each half into thirds. Place the potato wedges in a medium bowl, sprinkle with the rosemary, and toss with the avocado oil, salt, and pepper. Arrange the potatoes on a baking sheet in a single layer and bake for 40 minutes, or until golden brown, flipping them halfway through.

2. Prepare the beans. In a medium bowl, combine the beans, onion, cilantro, olive oil, lemon juice, garlic, salt, and pepper. Mix well. Taste and adjust the seasoning, if desired.

3. Prepare the salad. Massage the kale with the olive oil for a couple minutes by hand until it's tender and shiny. Add the carrot, apple, pepitas, lemon juice, salt, and pepper. Stir gently.

4. Assemble each bowl with half of the kale and apple salad, bean mixture, potato wedges, and avocado. Garnish with a lemon wedge and serve with the dressing.

Cashew-Cumin Dressing

Makes about ½ cup

¼ cup raw cashews, soaked in water for 30 minutes

¼ cup water

2 tablespoons freshly squeezed lime juice

2 tablespoons extra-virgin olive oil

Pinch of ground cumin

Pinch of sea salt

Pinch of freshly ground black pepper

- Rinse and drain the cashews. In a blender, combine the cashews, water, lime juice, oil, cumin, salt, and pepper. Blend on high for 1 to 2 minutes, until smooth and creamy, scraping down the sides as needed. Taste and adjust the seasoning, if desired.

INGREDIENTS

Roasted Cauliflower

4 cups cauliflower florets

2 tablespoons avocado oil

1 clove garlic, minced

¼ teaspoon sea salt

¼ teaspoon freshly ground black pepper

For Serving

2 cups kale, stemmed and finely chopped

1 cup shredded red cabbage

1 tablespoon extra-virgin olive oil

Pinch of sea salt

1 cup cooked quinoa (page 194)

1 cup cooked black beans (page 192)

1 medium avocado, sliced

¼ cup toasted pistachios, roughly chopped

½ cup Creamy Basil Pesto (page 53)

Warming Cauliflower & Quinoa Bowl with Creamy Basil Pesto

Roasted cauliflower tossed with oil and garlic is the centerpiece of this well-rounded bowl. While cauliflower is available year-round, its peak season is during the fall. Since it has a subtle, versatile taste, it pairs well with the bigger flavors here, like pistachios and pesto. Quinoa, black beans, and fresh kale make this a filling meal.

Makes 2 bowls

1. Prepare the cauliflower. Preheat the oven to 400 degrees F. In a medium bowl, toss the cauliflower, avocado oil, garlic, salt, and pepper. Spread the cauliflower florets in a single layer on a baking sheet. Roast for 30 minutes, flipping them halfway through, until they start to brown.

2. Massage the kale and cabbage with the olive oil and salt for a couple minutes by hand until they're shiny and soft.

3. Assemble each bowl with half of the roasted cauliflower, kale and cabbage, quinoa, black beans, avocado, and pistachios. Drizzle with the dressing.

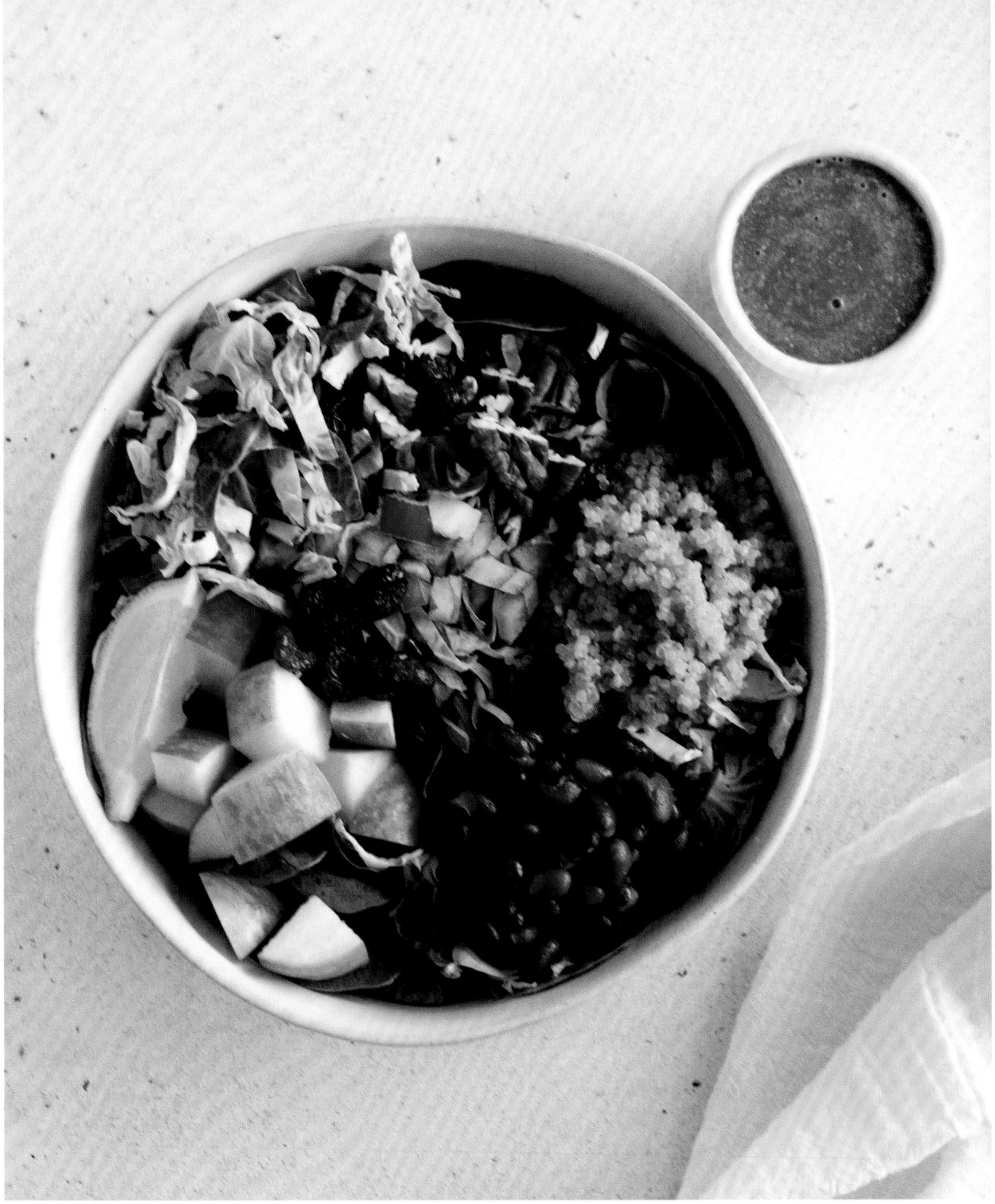

INGREDIENTS

2 cups spinach, roughly chopped
2 cups cooked quinoa (page 194)
2 cups cooked black beans (page 192)
1 cup thinly sliced brussels sprouts
1 medium red apple, diced
¼ cup diced red onion
2 tablespoons dried cranberries
2 tablespoons toasted pecans, roughly chopped
½ medium lemon, halved
½ cup Cilantro-Lime Dressing (page 65)

Autumn Chopped Salad Bowl

with Cilantro-Lime Dressing

Though I love to cozy up with a good roasted vegetable bowl, sometimes I just crave a refreshing, substantial salad. This bowl is crisp and delicious, with cranberries and juicy apples, crunchy raw brussels sprouts, and warming toasted pecans, all drizzled with a creamy dressing. It packs up nicely for a fall picnic, if you're so inclined—simply wait to dress the salad until just before eating.

Makes 2 bowls

1. Assemble each bowl with half of the spinach, quinoa, black beans, brussels sprouts, apple, red onion, cranberries, and pecans.
2. Garnish with a lemon wedge and serve with the dressing.

INGREDIENTS

1 sweet potato (about 5 ounces), peeled and diced

1 tablespoon avocado oil

Pinch of sea salt

Pinch of freshly ground black pepper

2 cups cooked quinoa (page 194)

2 cups cooked chickpeas (page 192)

1 cup shredded brussels sprouts

1 cup shredded red cabbage

1 medium carrot, julienned

½ medium yellow bell pepper, thinly sliced

½ cup roughly chopped fresh cilantro

¼ cup pomegranate seeds

½ cup Lemon-Tahini Dressing (page 71)

Rainbow Quinoa Bowl

with Lemon-Tahini Dressing

This bowl offers as much a feast for your eyes as it does for your body: the vibrant colors pull you right in and help you forget about the chill outside. You can style it like a literal rainbow in your bowl or toss the ingredients together to get a little bit of everything in each bite. Either way, you'll reap plenty of benefits from the many vitamins and antioxidants the dish has to offer.

Makes 2 bowls

1. Prepare the sweet potatoes. Preheat the oven to 325 degrees F. In a medium bowl, toss the sweet potato, oil, salt, and pepper. Spread in a single layer on a baking sheet and roast for 40 minutes, flipping them halfway through, until they start to brown slightly.

2. Assemble each bowl with half of the quinoa, chickpeas, brussels sprouts, cabbage, carrot, bell pepper, cilantro, and pomegranate seeds. Drizzle with the dressing.

Note

If you're not a fan of cilantro, Lemon-Tahini Dressing (page 71) works really well in place of the chutney.

INGREDIENTS

Curried Cauliflower

3 cups cauliflower florets

1 tablespoon avocado oil

¼ teaspoon ground turmeric

¼ teaspoon ground cumin

¼ teaspoon ground coriander

¼ teaspoon ground sweet paprika

¼ teaspoon chili powder

¼ teaspoon sea salt

¼ teaspoon freshly ground black pepper

For Serving

2 cups arugula

2 cups cooked black beans (page 192)

1 cup cooked quinoa (page 194)

1 medium avocado, sliced

2 tablespoons thinly sliced green onion (green parts only)

1 teaspoon toasted sesame seeds

½ medium lime, halved

½ cup Cilantro Chutney (page 18)

Curried Cauliflower Bowl

with Cilantro Chutney

Here, cauliflower is roasted with a medley of spices to create depth of flavor and warmth. It pairs especially well with the black beans, but you could swap in chickpeas or cannellini beans instead, if you want to change things up.

Makes 2 bowls

1. Prepare the cauliflower. Preheat the oven to 425 degrees F. In a medium bowl, toss the cauliflower florets, oil, turmeric, cumin, coriander, paprika, chili powder, salt, and pepper. Spread in a single layer on a baking sheet and roast for about 25 minutes, flipping them halfway through.

2. Assemble each bowl with half of the arugula, curried cauliflower, black beans, quinoa, avocado, and green onion. Sprinkle with the sesame seeds and garnish with a lime wedge. Serve with the chutney.

INGREDIENTS

6 ounces buckwheat soba noodles

2 cups finely chopped stemmed kale

1 tablespoon extra-virgin olive oil

Pinch of sea salt

1 medium avocado, sliced

¼ cup thinly sliced red bell pepper

¼ cup thinly sliced red cabbage

¼ cup julienned or shredded carrot

¼ cup julienned zucchini

¼ cup toasted peanuts or almonds

2 tablespoons sliced green onion (green parts only)

1 tablespoon toasted sesame seeds

½ cup Spicy Nut Dressing (page 27)

¼ cup chopped fresh cilantro

½ medium lime, halved

Buckwheat Soba Bowl

with Spicy Nut Dressing

I was inspired to create this bowl when I was craving sweet and spicy noodles. The vibrant red and green vegetables look beautiful alongside the buckwheat soba noodles, and what's more, the combination is versatile. Buckwheat soba noodles are made from buckwheat flour, which—despite the confusing name—is naturally gluten-free. Note that some commercial brands use a combination of buckwheat and wheat flours, so don't assume it is gluten-free by default. Feel free to swap out for another kind of noodle, such as udon or ramen, if gluten isn't a concern for you.

Makes 2 bowls

1. Follow the directions on the noodle package to cook the noodles. Drain well.

2. While the noodles cook, in a medium bowl, combine the kale, oil, and salt. Massage the kale with the oil for a couple minutes by hand, until it's tender and shiny.

3. Assemble each bowl with half of the noodles, kale, avocado, bell pepper, cabbage, carrot, zucchini, peanuts, green onion, and sesame seeds. Drizzle with the dressing. Taste and adjust the seasoning, if desired. Garnish with fresh cilantro and a lime wedge.

INGREDIENTS

Crispy Potatoes

3 medium Yukon Gold potatoes (about 1 pound), peeled and thinly sliced

1 tablespoon avocado oil

¼ teaspoon sea salt

Pinch of freshly ground black pepper

For Serving

2 cups cooked black beans (page 192)

1 medium avocado, diced

1 medium tomato, diced

¼ cup chopped fresh cilantro

¼ cup diced red onion

¼ cup fresh corn kernels

1 jalapeño pepper, seeded and sliced

½ cup Cashew Cheese Dressing (recipe follows)

Crispy Potato Nacho Bowl

with Cashew Cheese Dressing

You really can't go wrong with a bowl filled with potatoes and "cheese," right? This recipe is a great candidate for game or movie night—double or triple the ingredients, and invite friends over to build their own custom versions. You can either layer the ingredients as you would when making nachos or arrange them in side-by-side portions like a traditional Buddha bowl.

Makes 2 bowls

1. Prepare the potatoes. Preheat the oven to 425 degrees F. In a medium bowl, toss the potatoes, oil, salt, and pepper. Arrange in a single layer on a baking sheet. Bake for about 30 minutes, flipping them halfway through, until they are golden brown.

2. Assemble each bowl by layering half of the roasted potatoes, black beans, avocado, tomato, cilantro, onion, corn, and jalapeño. Drizzle with the dressing.

Cashew Cheese Dressing

Makes about ½ cup

¼ cup raw cashews, soaked in water for 30 minutes
¼ cup water
1 tablespoon nutritional yeast
1½ teaspoons freshly squeezed lemon juice
1 clove garlic, minced
Pinch of sea salt

- Rinse and drain the cashews. In a blender, combine the cashews, water, yeast, lemon juice, garlic, and salt. Blend on high for 1 to 2 minutes, until smooth and creamy, scraping down the sides as needed. Taste and adjust the seasoning, if desired.

Crispy Potato Nacho Bowl
(page 102)

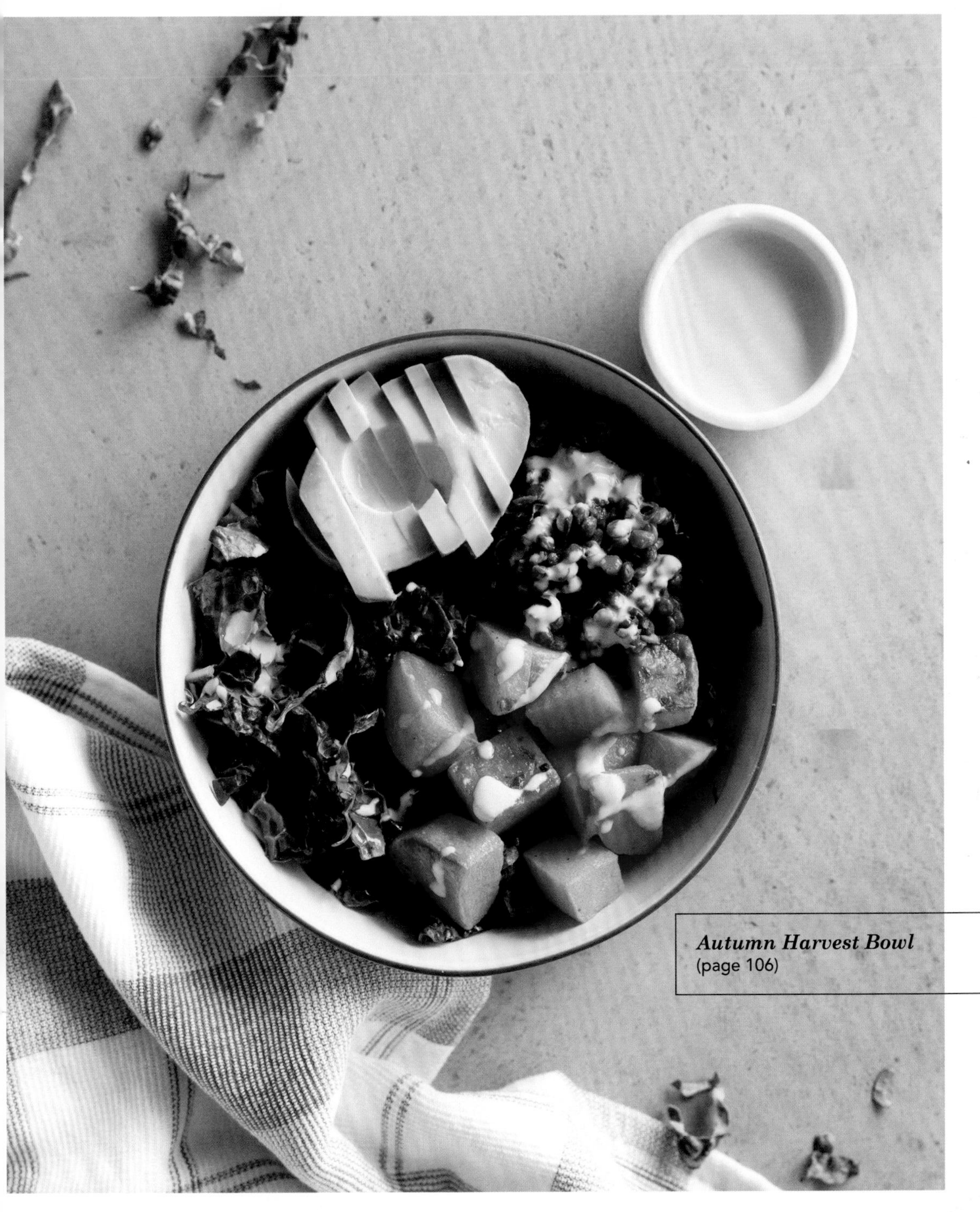

Autumn Harvest Bowl
(page 106)

INGREDIENTS

Roasted Butternut Squash

3 cups cubed peeled butternut squash

1 tablespoon avocado oil

1 teaspoon ground cinnamon

¼ teaspoon sea salt

For Serving

2 cups thinly sliced stemmed kale

1 tablespoon extra-virgin olive oil

2 cups cooked lentils (page 193)

1 medium avocado, sliced

½ cup Ginger-Lime-Walnut Dressing (recipe follows)

Autumn Harvest Bowl

with Ginger-Lime-Walnut Dressing

This satisfying bowl is filled with greens and packed with flavor, plus the pairing of the roasted butternut squash and the lentils will warm you up. It's a quick and easy meal to pull together any day of the week.

Makes 2 bowls

1. Prepare the butternut squash. Preheat the oven to 400 degrees F. In a medium bowl, toss the squash, avocado oil, cinnamon, and salt. Spread the cubes in a single layer on a baking sheet and roast until they're tender, about 25 minutes. Remove them from the oven and let cool down.

2. Massage the kale with the olive oil for a couple minutes by hand, until it's tender and shiny.

3. Assemble each bowl with half of the squash, kale, lentils, and avocado. Drizzle with the dressing.

Ginger-Lime-Walnut Dressing

Makes about ½ cup

¼ cup raw walnuts, soaked in water for 30 minutes
¼ cup water
2 tablespoons extra-virgin olive oil
1 tablespoon freshly squeezed lime juice
½ teaspoon grated peeled fresh ginger
Pinch of sea salt

- Rinse and drain the walnuts. In a blender, combine the walnuts, water, oil, lime juice, ginger, and salt. Blend on high for about 1 minute, until smooth and creamy, scraping down the sides as needed. Taste and adjust the seasoning, if desired.

INGREDIENTS

Roasted Beets

2 medium beets, peeled and quartered

1 clove garlic, minced

1 tablespoon avocado oil

¼ teaspoon freshly ground black pepper

¼ teaspoon sea salt

1 tablespoon freshly squeezed lemon juice

For Serving

3 cups thinly sliced brussels sprouts

2 cups cooked quinoa (page 194)

2 cups cooked chickpeas (page 192)

¼ cup chopped toasted pecans

½ cup Cranberry-Tahini Dressing (recipe follows)

Shaved Brussels Sprout & Roasted Beet Bowl with Cranberry-Tahini Dressing

This bowl is a powerhouse of nutrition. Brussels sprouts, which taste great raw when thinly sliced or shredded, are hearty and high in fiber, antioxidants, and vitamins K and C. Beets are a good source of vitamin C as well, plus iron and fiber. The rich and sweet-tart dressing makes this is a fabulous dish to add to your Thanksgiving table, whether or not you or your guests are vegan.

Makes 2 bowls

1. Prepare the beets. Preheat the oven to 400 degrees F. In a medium bowl, toss the beets, garlic, oil, and salt. Wrap the beets in aluminum foil and place them on a baking sheet. Roast for 30 to 45 minutes, until the beets are tender (stick a toothpick or fork into them to make sure). Remove from the oven and drizzle with the lemon juice. Taste and adjust the seasoning, if desired.

Continued on next page

2. Meanwhile, in a large bowl, combine the brussels sprouts, quinoa, chickpeas, and pecans and toss together.

3. Stir the roasted beets into the brussels sprout mixture, then divide between two bowls. Serve with the dressing.

Cranberry-Tahini Dressing

Makes about ½ cup

2 tablespoons dried cranberries, soaked in water for 30 minutes
¼ cup tahini
¼ cup water
1 tablespoon freshly squeezed lemon juice
1 tablespoon extra-virgin olive oil
1 teaspoon pure maple syrup
1 clove garlic, minced
½ teaspoon ground cumin
Pinch of sea salt
Pinch of freshly ground black pepper

- Rinse and drain the cranberries. In a blender, combine the cranberries, tahini, water, lemon juice, oil, maple syrup, garlic, cumin, salt, and pepper. Blend on high for about 1 minute, until smooth and creamy, scraping down the sides as needed. Taste and adjust the seasoning, if desired.

INGREDIENTS

Sautéed Eggplant

1 tablespoon avocado oil

¼ cup diced yellow onion

1 clove garlic, minced

1 medium eggplant (about 1¼ pounds), peeled and diced

½ teaspoon sea salt

¼ teaspoon freshly ground black pepper

Zucchini Salad

1 medium zucchini

¼ cup pepitas

1 tablespoon freshly squeezed lemon juice

1 tablespoon extra-virgin olive oil

Pinch of sea salt

Pinch of freshly ground black pepper

For Serving

2 cups cooked millet (page 196)

½ medium lemon, halved

½ cup Fig-Balsamic Vinaigrette (recipe follows)

Sautéed Eggplant & Millet Bowl

with Fig-Balsamic Vinaigrette

Millet is a heart-healthy ancient grain high in nutritional value and rich in amino acids; you can find it in the bulk section of any well-stocked natural food store. In this bowl, the tender eggplant is cooked in onion and garlic to create a rich flavor. The fig and balsamic dressing adds sweetness, and the zucchini salad offers a crisp crunch to help balance the eggplant's soft texture.

Makes 2 bowls

1. Prepare the eggplant. In a medium skillet over low heat, warm the avocado oil. Add the onion and stir to coat. Cook for about 5 minutes, until

Continued on next page

it becomes translucent. Increase the heat to medium and add the garlic, eggplant, salt, and pepper. Cook for 10 to 15 minutes, until the eggplant is tender.

2. Prepare the zucchini salad. Shave the zucchini lengthwise with a vegetable peeler. In a medium bowl, toss the zucchini, pepitas, lemon juice, olive oil, salt, and pepper.

3. Assemble each bowl with half of the millet, zucchini salad, and sautéed eggplant. Garnish with a lemon wedge and serve with the dressing.

Fig-Balsamic Vinaigrette

Makes about ½ cup

2 fresh figs
¼ cup extra-virgin olive oil
2 tablespoons balsamic vinegar
Pinch of sea salt
Pinch of freshly ground black pepper

- In a blender, combine the figs, oil, vinegar, salt, and pepper. Blend on high for about 1 minute, until smooth and creamy, scraping down the sides as needed. Taste and adjust the seasoning, if desired.

INGREDIENTS

Cauliflower & Butternut Squash Korma

1 tablespoon avocado oil

¼ cup diced yellow onion

1 clove garlic, minced

½ teaspoon ground cumin

½ teaspoon ground turmeric

½ teaspoon chili powder

3 cups cauliflower florets

3 cups cubed peeled butternut squash

2 cups spinach, roughly chopped

1 cup full-fat coconut milk

For Serving

2 cups cooked brown or white rice (page 195)

¼ cup toasted cashews, roughly chopped

¼ cup fresh cilantro leaves

½ medium lemon, halved

½ cup Cilantro Chutney (page 18)

Cauliflower & Butternut Squash Korma Bowl with Cilantro Chutney

This Indian-inspired bowl is rich in flavor, mildly spiced, and easy to make. In Urdu, *korma* means "to braise" and refers to the cooking technique used here: the vegetables are simmered in coconut milk and spices until a thickened consistency is achieved. The rich, hearty, and warming korma is then served over rice and topped with crunchy cashews and vibrant cilantro chutney.

Makes 2 bowls

1. Prepare the korma. In a large pot over low heat, warm the oil. Add the onion and garlic and cook until the onion starts to appear translucent, about 5 minutes. Add the cumin, turmeric, and chili powder. Sauté for

a few minutes, then increase the heat to medium. Add the cauliflower, squash, and spinach and stir. Add the coconut milk and increase the heat to bring the mixture to a boil. Immediately reduce the heat to low, cover, and let simmer for about 30 minutes, until the squash is tender.

2. Assemble each bowl with half of the rice, korma, and cashews. Garnish with the cilantro and a lemon wedge. Serve with the chutney.

INGREDIENTS

Roasted Pumpkin

½ small sugar pumpkin (about 1½ pounds), peeled, seeded, and cut into 1-inch pieces

1 tablespoon avocado oil

1 teaspoon ground cinnamon

½ teaspoon ground sweet paprika

¼ teaspoon sea salt

¼ teaspoon freshly ground black pepper

For Serving

2 cups cooked quinoa (page 194)

2 cups cooked chickpeas (page 192)

2 cups arugula

¼ cup thinly sliced red onion

½ cup raw almonds, roughly chopped

½ cup Lemon-Tahini Dressing (page 71)

Quinoa & Pumpkin Bowl

with Lemon-Tahini Dressing

You know it's fall when you start seeing pumpkins for sale everywhere—and not only the large, decorative ones used to make jack-o'-lanterns for Halloween. The smaller varieties are known as sugar or pie pumpkins, and they make a delicious addition to your bowl. They are especially great roasted with a little spice and paired with quinoa.

Makes 2 bowls

1. Prepare the pumpkin. Preheat the oven to 425 degrees F. In a large bowl, toss the pumpkin, oil, cinnamon, paprika, salt, and pepper. Spread in a single layer on a baking sheet and roast for about 30 minutes, flipping the pumpkin halfway through, until it is soft.

2. Assemble each bowl with half of the roasted pumpkin, quinoa, chickpeas, arugula, onion, and almonds. Drizzle with the dressing.

INGREDIENTS

Steamed Carrots

2 medium carrots, peeled and diced

2 tablespoons finely minced fresh parsley

1 tablespoon extra-virgin olive oil

¼ teaspoon sea salt

¼ teaspoon freshly ground black pepper

For Serving

2 cups thinly sliced stemmed kale

1 tablespoon extra-virgin olive oil

2 cups cooked buckwheat (page 197)

1 cup shredded red cabbage

1 medium avocado, sliced

2 tablespoons finely diced red onion

½ medium lemon, halved

½ cup Creamy Cashew Dressing (page 59)

Kale & Carrot Buckwheat Bowl

with Creamy Cashew Dressing

Buckwheat is a great source of fiber, antioxidants, and minerals—magnesium in particular. It's also naturally gluten-free and anti-inflammatory. Here, it pairs well with kale, cabbage, seasoned carrots, and a creamy cashew dressing for the ultimate in comfort food.

Makes 2 bowls

1. Prepare the carrots. Bring a pot of water with a steamer insert to a boil. Place the carrots in the basket and steam for about 10 minutes, until tender. Transfer to a small bowl and combine with the parsley, oil, salt, and pepper.

2. In a medium bowl, massage the kale with the oil for a couple minutes by hand, until it's tender and shiny.

3. Assemble each bowl with half of the carrots, kale, buckwheat, cabbage, avocado, and onion. Garnish with a lemon wedge and drizzle with the dressing.

INGREDIENTS

Roasted Sweet Potatoes

2 sweet potatoes (about 10 ounces), peeled and diced

1 tablespoon avocado oil

¼ teaspoon sea salt

¼ teaspoon freshly ground black pepper

Spiced Chickpeas

1 tablespoon avocado oil

2 cups cooked chickpeas (page 192)

1 teaspoon ground sweet paprika

1 teaspoon ground cumin

¼ teaspoon ground turmeric

¼ teaspoon sea salt

¼ teaspoon freshly ground black pepper

Pinch of cayenne pepper

For Serving

2 cups arugula

2 cups cooked farro (page 197)

¼ cup toasted pecans, roughly chopped

¼ cup diced red onion

½ cup Cucumber-Dill Dressing (page 42)

Sweet Potato & Farro Bowl

with Cucumber-Dill Dressing

Farro is a nutritious, ancient whole grain that tastes similar to brown rice—and has a similar chewy texture. It is an excellent source of fiber and is full of protein, vitamins, antioxidants, and essential minerals. When buying farro, be sure to seek out the pearled kind, as it requires less cooking time. The nutty farro pairs well with the sweet potatoes.

Makes 2 bowls

1. Prepare the sweet potatoes. Preheat the oven to 375 degrees F. In a large bowl, toss the sweet potatoes, oil, salt, and black pepper. Spread in a single layer on a baking sheet and roast for 40 minutes, flipping them halfway through, until they start to brown.

2. Prepare the chickpeas. In a medium skillet over medium heat, warm the oil. Add the chickpeas, paprika, cumin, turmeric, salt, black pepper, and cayenne.

3. Assemble each bowl with half of the arugula, farro, roasted sweet potatoes, spiced chickpeas, pecans, and onion. Serve with the dressing.

INGREDIENTS

Roasted Vegetables

1 delicata squash, cut into ½-inch-thick slices and seeded

2 cups halved brussels sprouts

1 tablespoon avocado oil

Pinch of sea salt

Pinch of freshly ground black pepper

For Serving

2 cups kale, stemmed and torn into bite-size pieces

1 tablespoon extra-virgin olive oil

1 cup cooked quinoa (page 194)

½ cup pomegranate seeds

2 tablespoons minced fresh mint

½ cup Cashew Cheese Dressing (page 103)

Fall Harvest Squash Bowl

with Cashew Cheese Dressing

This bowl highlights many of fall's peak-season ingredients and brings out their best qualities: delicata squash and brussels sprouts are roasted at high heat for maximum flavor. Pomegranate seeds add a pop of color and a burst of sweet flavor. Together they make for an energizing, sweet, and savory bowl.

Makes 2 bowls

1. Prepare the roasted vegetables. Preheat the oven to 400 degrees F. In a large bowl, toss the squash, brussels sprouts, avocado oil, salt, and pepper. Arrange in a single layer on a baking sheet and roast for 45 minutes, flipping them halfway through, until slightly browned.

2. In a medium bowl, combine the kale and olive oil. Massage the kale with the oil for a couple minutes by hand, until it's tender and shiny.

3. Assemble each bowl with half of the kale, quinoa, roasted vegetables, pomegranate seeds, and mint. Serve with the dressing.

Winter Bowls

Roasted Beet & Spicy Lentil Bowl (page 128)

Winter is a good time to boost the protein and fat content in our diet to help keep our bodies warm and nourished. Since it is natural to spend more time at home during this season, use this opportunity to dig through the kitchen pantry and see what you need to stock up on for the cold months ahead.

When fresh produce is limited and many farmers' markets are closed, it's nice to have a wide selection of nuts and nut butters, seeds, oils, grains, beans and lentils, and spices on hand for variety. One of my own favorite ways to embrace winter is by using cinnamon, ginger, cumin, fennel, and cloves in my cooking.

When I first started cooking seasonally, I didn't realize the variety of produce that is at its peak in the cold months, such as hearty greens, leeks, brussels sprouts, turnips, and squash. These ingredients make it a lot easier to feel our best, despite the cold and wet months, as we wait for spring to arrive again.

INGREDIENTS

Roasted Beets

2 medium beets, peeled and quartered

1 tablespoon avocado oil

1 clove garlic, minced

¼ teaspoon sea salt

1 tablespoon freshly squeezed lemon juice

Spicy Lentils

1 tablespoon avocado oil

¼ cup diced yellow onion

1 clove garlic, minced

½ teaspoon ground cumin

½ teaspoon ground sweet paprika

½ teaspoon chili powder

½ teaspoon ground turmeric

½ teaspoon sea salt

¼ teaspoon freshly ground black pepper

2 cups cooked lentils (page 193)

¼ cup water

For Serving

1 cup cooked millet (page 196)

1 medium avocado, sliced

½ cup diced carrot

½ cup chopped fresh cilantro

½ medium lemon, halved

½ cup Creamy Turmeric Dressing (page 82)

Roasted Beet & Spicy Lentil Bowl

with Creamy Turmeric Dressing

I've been eating lentils for as long as I can remember. In the vegetarian Indian household I grew up in, lentils were a key staple. These lentils use my go-to technique for enjoying them: cooking them as a stew in warming Indian spices. This dish is also a great candidate for food prep day, as lentils taste delicious and store well for a few days.

Makes 2 bowls

1. Prepare the beets. Preheat the oven to 400 degrees F. In a medium bowl, toss the beets, oil, garlic, and salt. Wrap the beets in aluminum foil and place them on a baking sheet. Roast for 30 to 45 minutes, until the beets are tender (stick a toothpick or fork into them to make sure). Remove from the oven and drizzle with the lemon juice. Taste and adjust the seasoning, if desired.
2. Prepare the lentils. In a medium pot over medium heat, warm the oil. Add the onion and stir. Cook for about 5 minutes, until the onion appears translucent. Add the garlic, cumin, paprika, chili powder, turmeric, salt, and pepper. Cook for a minute, until the spices are fragrant. Add the lentils and water, stir, and cover. Simmer for 15 minutes, stirring frequently.
3. Assemble each bowl with half of the roasted beets, spicy lentils, millet, avocado, carrot, and cilantro. Garnish with a lemon wedge and drizzle with the dressing.

INGREDIENTS

Brussels Sprouts & Squash

2 cups halved brussels sprouts

2 cups diced peeled butternut squash

2 tablespoons avocado oil

1 tablespoon minced fresh thyme, or 1 teaspoon dried

¼ teaspoon sea salt

¼ teaspoon freshly ground black pepper

Cannellini Beans

1 tablespoon avocado oil

1 clove garlic, minced

2 cups cooked cannellini beans (page 192)

¼ teaspoon sea salt

¼ teaspoon freshly ground black pepper

For Serving

2 cups roughly chopped spinach

1 medium avocado, sliced

¼ cup dried cranberries

½ cup Almond-Ginger Dressing (page 85)

Crispy Brussels Sprout & Winter Squash Bowl with Almond-Ginger Dressing

This bowl brings two of winter's best offerings together: here, the delicate sweetness of butternut squash balances the nutty, savory taste of brussels sprouts. Combining them with cannellini beans and spinach makes for a fantastically filling, seasonal meal and a good candidate for holiday potlucks.

Makes 2 bowls

1. Prepare the brussels sprouts and squash. Preheat the oven to 450 degrees F. In a large bowl, toss the brussels sprouts, squash, oil, thyme, salt, and pepper. Arrange the sprouts facedown on a baking sheet in a single layer alongside the squash. Roast for about 40 minutes, flipping them halfway through, until they start to brown.

2. Prepare the beans. In a medium skillet over low heat, warm the oil. Add the garlic and stir for a few minutes until it's fragrant and slightly transparent. Increase the heat to medium and add the beans, salt, and pepper. Cook for 5 minutes, or until the beans are warm and cooked through.

3. Assemble each bowl with half of the spinach, brussels sprouts and squash, beans, avocado, and cranberries. Drizzle with the dressing.

INGREDIENTS

Cauliflower-Chickpea Curry

1 tablespoon avocado oil

¼ cup diced yellow onion

1 clove garlic, minced

2 cups cooked chickpeas (page 192)

1 cup cauliflower florets

¼ cup water

1 teaspoon ground sweet paprika

1 teaspoon ground cumin

½ teaspoon ground turmeric

½ teaspoon ground cinnamon

¼ teaspoon sea salt

¼ teaspoon freshly ground black pepper

For Serving

2 cups shredded radicchio

1 cup shredded or thinly sliced red cabbage

1 medium carrot, shaved into ribbons using a peeler or mandoline (about 1 cup)

1 medium avocado, halved

1 jalapeño pepper, seeded and sliced (optional)

½ medium lemon, halved

½ cup Spicy Cashew Dressing (recipe follows)

Cauliflower-Chickpea Curry & Avocado Bowl with Spicy Cashew Dressing

This bowl makes for a simple yet utterly satisfying weeknight dinner. Better yet, the recipe is infinitely customizable based on whatever you have in the refrigerator, so experiment with using broccoli instead of cauliflower or spinach instead of radicchio—or add seeds or nuts.

Makes 2 bowls

1. Prepare the cauliflower-chickpea curry. In a large pot over low heat, warm the oil. Add the onion and garlic. Stir occasionally until the onion starts to get soft and translucent, about 5 minutes. Add the chickpeas, cauliflower,

water, paprika, cumin, turmeric, cinnamon, salt, and pepper. Stir until the cauliflower is well coated. Increase the heat to medium and cover. Cook for about 30 minutes, stirring occasionally.

2. Assemble each bowl with half of the radicchio, cauliflower-chickpea curry, cabbage, carrot, avocado, and jalapeño. Garnish with a lemon wedge and serve with the dressing.

Spicy Cashew Dressing

Makes about ½ cup

¼ cup raw cashews, soaked in water for 30 minutes
¼ cup water
1 tablespoon freshly squeezed lime juice
½ teaspoon chili powder
Dash of cayenne pepper
Pinch of sea salt

- Rinse and drain the cashews. In a blender, combine the cashews, water, lime juice, chili powder, cayenne, and salt. Blend on high for about 1 minute, until smooth and creamy, scraping down the sides as needed. Taste and adjust the seasoning, if desired.

Cauliflower-Chickpea Curry & Avocado Bowl (page 132)

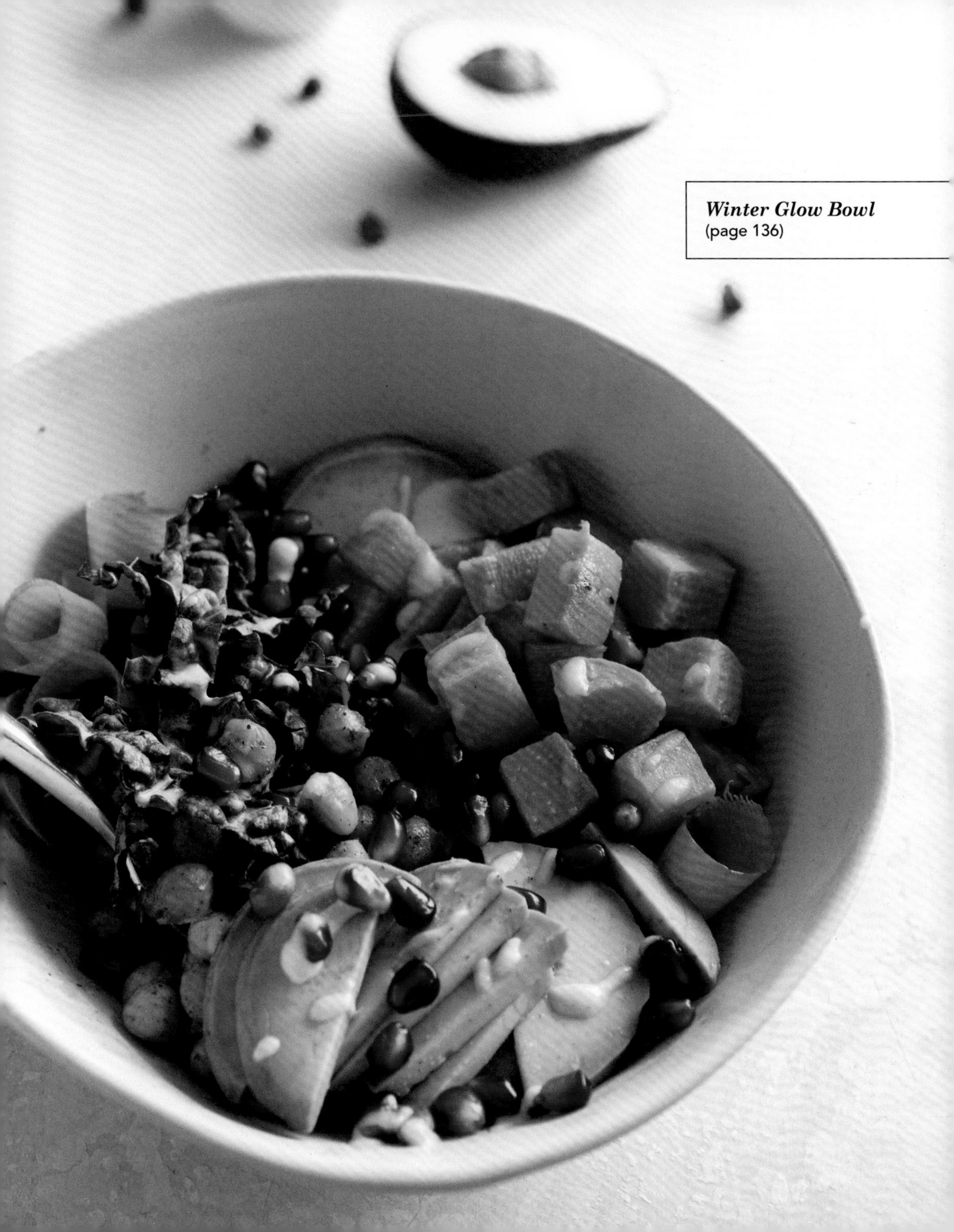

Winter Glow Bowl
(page 136)

INGREDIENTS

Roasted Sweet Potatoes

2 sweet potatoes (about 10 ounces), peeled and cubed

1 tablespoon avocado oil

¼ teaspoon sea salt

¼ teaspoon freshly ground black pepper

Chickpeas

1 tablespoon avocado oil

2 cups cooked chickpeas (page 192)

¼ teaspoon ground cumin

¼ teaspoon ground turmeric

½ teaspoon ground sweet paprika

¼ teaspoon sea salt

¼ teaspoon freshly ground black pepper

For Serving

2 cups kale, stemmed and chopped

1 teaspoon extra-virgin olive oil

Pinch of sea salt

1 medium carrot, shaved into ribbons using a peeler or mandoline (about 1 cup)

1 medium avocado, sliced

¼ cup pomegranate seeds

½ cup Lemon-Tahini Dressing (page 71)

Winter Glow Bowl

with Lemon-Tahini Dressing

This bowl is one of my personal favorites: thanks to the antioxidants in the pomegranate, it can promote healthy skin and prevent premature aging and wrinkles. Carrots, dark leafy greens, and sweet potatoes are rich in Vitamin A, making your skin glow, while the healthy fats in avocados can be your skin's best friend through the cooler months!

Makes 2 bowls

1. Prepare the sweet potatoes. Preheat the oven to 425 degrees F. In a medium bowl, combine the sweet potatoes, avocado oil, salt, and pepper. Toss until the potatoes are well coated in oil. Arrange the sweet potatoes in a single layer on a baking sheet. Roast for 30 minutes, flipping them halfway through, until they start to brown and crisp.

2. Prepare the chickpeas. In a medium skillet over medium heat, warm the avocado oil. Add the chickpeas, cumin, turmeric, paprika, salt, and pepper. Stir until the chickpeas are well coated. Cook for about 10 minutes, or until the chickpeas start to crisp and turn light golden brown. Set aside.

3. In a medium bowl, combine the kale and olive oil. With your hands, massage the kale with the oil for a couple minutes, or until it's tender and shiny. Taste and adjust the seasoning, if desired.

4. Assemble each bowl with half of the kale, chickpeas, roasted sweet potatoes, carrot, avocado, and pomegranate seeds. Drizzle with the dressing.

INGREDIENTS

Coconut-Chickpea Curry

1 tablespoon avocado oil

¼ cup diced yellow onion

2 cups cooked chickpeas (page 192)

½ teaspoon ground cumin

¼ teaspoon ground turmeric

¼ teaspoon ground cinnamon

1 clove garlic, minced

¼ teaspoon sea salt

¼ teaspoon freshly ground black pepper

¼ cup full-fat coconut milk

For Serving

2 cups broccoli florets

2 cups cooked brown or white rice (page 195)

½ cup Lemon-Tahini Dressing (page 71)

½ medium lemon, halved

Coconut-Chickpea Curry & Broccoli Bowl with Lemon-Tahini Dressing

Curries are typically made in one of two ways: using either a paste or a blend of ground spices. This recipe takes the latter approach, yet it's light enough on heat (and heavier on the coconut milk) to make it a great candidate for those with more sensitive taste buds.

Makes 2 bowls

1. Prepare the chickpea curry. In a medium pot over low heat, warm the oil. Add the onion and sauté until translucent, about 5 minutes. Add the chickpeas, cumin, turmeric, cinnamon, garlic, salt, and pepper. Cook for about 5 minutes, or until the spices are fragrant. Add the coconut milk

and stir to incorporate. Simmer gently for 20 minutes, or until the curry has thickened, then turn off heat.

2. Prepare the broccoli. Bring a pot of water with a steamer insert to a boil. Place the broccoli in the basket and steam for 7 minutes, or until the stems are fork-tender.

3. Assemble each bowl with half of the chickpea curry, broccoli, and rice. Drizzle with the dressing or serve it as a dipping sauce for the broccoli. Garnish with a lemon wedge.

INGREDIENTS

4 cups cubed peeled butternut squash
1 tablespoon avocado oil
1 teaspoon ground cinnamon
¼ teaspoon sea salt
¼ teaspoon freshly ground black pepper
4 cups thinly sliced spinach
2 cups cooked quinoa (page 194)
½ cup pomegranate seeds
¼ cup diced red onion
2 tablespoons minced fresh mint leaves
½ medium lemon, halved
½ cup Walnut-Kale Pesto (page 23)

Roasted Winter Squash & Pomegranate Bowl with Walnut-Kale Pesto

This sweet and savory bowl features butternut squash, spinach, and pomegranate and is perfect for warming up on a night in. The mint leaves add a hit of bright flavor, and the accompanying pesto is made with a twist, using kale and walnuts instead of the traditional basil and pine nuts to create a heartier dish.

Makes 2 bowls

1. Preheat the oven to 400 degrees F. In a large bowl, toss the squash, oil, cinnamon, salt, and pepper. Arrange the cubes in a single layer on baking sheet and roast until they're tender, about 25 minutes. Remove them from the oven and let cool down.

2. Assemble each bowl with half of the spinach, quinoa, pomegranate seeds, onion, roasted squash, and mint. Garnish with a lemon wedge and serve with the pesto.

INGREDIENTS

1 small beet, peeled

1 cup hummus (page 190)

Pinch of sea salt

2 big handfuls spinach, roughly chopped

2 cups cooked quinoa (page 194)

2 cups shelled edamame

½ red bell pepper, thinly sliced

1 medium carrot, shaved into ribbons using a peeler or mandoline (about 1 cup)

½ cup Almond-Ginger Dressing (page 85)

Weeknight Quinoa Bowl

with Beet Hummus & Almond-Ginger Dressing

This bowl makes for a quick and tasty weeknight meal. It's easy to pull together and contains energy-boosting vegetables and edamame for added protein. If you're not in the mood for using the oven to cook one beet, bake a bunch at once and use them throughout the week in other bowls. Alternatively, you could use one teaspoon beet powder or skip the beet altogether.

Makes 2 bowls

1. Preheat the oven to 400 degrees F. Wrap the beet in aluminum foil to create a little pouch. Place the pouch on a baking sheet and roast for about 45 minutes, until tender all the way through (stick a toothpick or fork into it to check). Remove it from the oven and let cool down before proceeding.

2. Once the beet is cool, in a blender or food processor, blend the beet, hummus, and salt on high for about 1 minute, until smooth and creamy, scraping down the sides as needed. Taste and adjust the seasoning, if desired.

3. Assemble each bowl with half of the spinach, quinoa, edamame, bell pepper, and carrot. Top with a dollop of beet hummus and serve with the dressing.

INGREDIENTS

Roasted Root Vegetables

1 cup diced carrot

1 medium sweet potato (about 5 ounces), peeled and diced

1 parsnip (about 4 ounces), peeled and diced

2 tablespoons avocado oil

1 clove garlic, minced

¼ teaspoon sea salt

¼ teaspoon freshly ground black pepper

Black Beans

2 cups cooked black beans (page 192)

½ cup chopped fresh cilantro

¼ cup diced red onion

¼ teaspoon sea salt

¼ teaspoon freshly ground black pepper

For Serving

2 cups cooked brown or white rice (page 195)

2 cups thinly sliced chard

½ cup Creamy Herb Dressing (page 7)

½ medium lemon, halved

Black Bean & Root Vegetable Bowl

with Creamy Herb Dressing

This bowl features a medley of energizing roasted root vegetables—carrot, sweet potato, and parsnip—combined with black beans and rice. The herb dressing brings all the flavors together. If you prepare the components in advance, this bowl comes together in less than ten minutes.

Makes 2 bowls

1. Prepare the root vegetables. Preheat the oven to 425 degrees F. In a large bowl, toss the carrot, sweet potato, parsnip, oil, garlic, salt, and pepper. Arrange the vegetables in a single layer on a baking sheet. Roast for about 30 minutes, flipping them halfway through, until lightly browned.

2. Prepare the beans. In a medium bowl, combine the beans, cilantro, onion, salt, and pepper.
3. Assemble each bowl with half of the rice, chard, beans, and root vegetables. Drizzle with the dressing and garnish with a lemon wedge.

INGREDIENTS

Chickpea-Coconut Curry

1 tablespoon avocado oil

1 cup diced tomato

½ cup diced yellow onion

2 cups cooked chickpeas (page 192)

2 cups broccoli florets

1 (12-ounce) can full-fat coconut milk

¼ cup chopped fresh cilantro

1 teaspoon curry powder

1 clove garlic, minced

¼ teaspoon cayenne pepper

¼ teaspoon sea salt

¼ teaspoon freshly ground black pepper

For Serving

2 cups cooked white or brown rice (page 195)

¼ cup chopped fresh cilantro

½ medium lime, halved

Warming Chickpea-Coconut Curry Bowl

This bowl hits all the comfort-food buttons but in a good-for-you way. While the key spice is curry powder, if you don't have any on hand, you can simply use one-quarter teaspoon each of ground cumin, turmeric, cinnamon, and coriander instead. The broccoli adds texture and loads of benefits, including a major dose of folic acid and vitamin C.

Makes 2 bowls

1. Prepare the chickpea curry. In a medium pot over medium heat, warm the oil. Add the tomato and onion and cook for about 3 minutes, until the onion is translucent, stirring occasionally. Add the chickpeas, broccoli, coconut milk, cilantro, curry powder, garlic, cayenne, salt, and black pepper. Bring to a boil, reduce the heat to medium-low, and simmer the curry for about 25 minutes.

2. Assemble each bowl with half of the rice, chickpea curry, and cilantro. Garnish with a lime wedge.

INGREDIENTS

Cucumber Salad

2 cups diced cucumber

1 cup diced tomato

½ cup diced red bell pepper

¼ cup diced red onion

¼ cup chopped fresh parsley

1 tablespoon freshly squeezed lemon juice

¼ teaspoon sea salt

Za'atar Chickpeas

2 cups cooked chickpeas (page 192)

1 teaspoon za'atar

1 teaspoon ground cumin

¼ teaspoon sea salt

¼ teaspoon freshly ground black pepper

For Serving

2 cups cooked quinoa (page 194)

¼ cup pitted kalamata olives

½ medium lemon, halved

½ cup Lemon-Tahini Dressing (page 71)

Za'atar Quinoa Bowl

with Lemon-Tahini Dressing

This bowl takes a break from heavier winter meals. It's infused with Mediterranean flavors through the use of ingredients such as za'atar, tahini, and parsley. Za'atar is a blend of fresh herbs that includes thyme and marjoram—in Arabic, the word *za'atar* means "thyme." Many natural food stores sell this in their spice or bulk section, but if you have a hard time finding it, you can make your own blend (see the accompanying sidebar). Remember: the fresher the dried herbs, the more aromatic your za'atar will be.

Makes 2 bowls

1. Prepare the cucumber salad. In a medium bowl, combine the cucumber, tomato, bell pepper, onion, parsley, lemon juice, and salt. Mix well.

2. Prepare the chickpeas. In a medium bowl, combine chickpeas, za'atar, cumin, salt, and pepper. Mix well.

3. Assemble each bowl with half of the cucumber salad, chickpeas, quinoa, and olives. Garnish with a lemon wedge and serve with the dressing.

Homemade Za'atar Blend

Makes about ½ cup

1 tablespoon dried thyme
1 tablespoon dried marjoram
1 tablespoon toasted sesame seeds
1 tablespoon ground sumac
¼ teaspoon sea salt

In a small bowl, combine the thyme, marjoram, sesame seeds, sumac, and salt. Mix well. Leftover za'atar can be stored in an airtight container in the pantry or refrigerator for up to 3 months.

INGREDIENTS

2 sweet potatoes (about 10 ounces), peeled
2 tablespoons avocado oil
½ teaspoon sea salt
½ teaspoon freshly ground black pepper
2 cups cooked black beans (page 192)
2 cups cooked quinoa (page 194)
2 cups roughly chopped chard
½ cup chopped fresh cilantro
¼ cup diced red onion
1 medium avocado, sliced
½ cup Creamy Cashew Dressing (page 59)

Power Macro Bowl

with Sweet Potato Fries & Creamy Cashew Dressing

What I love most about this bowl is the addition of sweet potato fries. Homemade fries are an easy way to include something crisp and savory in a bowl. You could also just make them on their own and use the creamy cashew dressing as a dip. Pairing them with the black beans and quinoa as a meal, however, will fill you up and provide a powerful energy boost.

Makes 2 bowls

1. Prepare the fries. Preheat the oven to 450 degrees F. Cut the sweet potatoes into 4-inch-long sticks. In a large bowl, toss the sweet potatoes, oil, salt, and pepper. Arrange in a single layer on a baking sheet and bake for 15 minutes, then flip. Bake for another 20 minutes until they are lightly browned, making sure they don't overcook.

2. Assemble each bowl with half of the beans, quinoa, chard, cilantro, onion, avocado, and fries. Drizzle with the dressing.

INGREDIENTS

Roasted Sweet Potatoes

2 sweet potatoes (about 10 ounces), peeled and cubed

1 tablespoon avocado oil

¼ teaspoon sea salt

¼ teaspoon freshly ground black pepper

For Serving

2 handfuls arugula

2 cups cooked chickpeas (page 192)

2 cups cooked pearl barley (page 196)

1 cup thinly sliced red cabbage

1 medium avocado, sliced

½ cup Matcha-Cashew Dressing (recipe follows)

Mighty Green Macro Bowl
with Matcha-Cashew Dressing

Matcha is a special type of finely ground caffeinated green tea from Japan. Unlike other teas, matcha isn't strained before you consume it. It contains a high concentration of antioxidants as well as the amino acid theanine, which is known to support focus and concentration. The dressing that accompanies this bowl is a perfect example of how to incorporate matcha without letting it overpower other ingredients.

Makes 2 bowls

1. Prepare the sweet potatoes. Preheat the oven to 425 degrees F. In a medium bowl, combine the sweet potatoes, oil, salt, and pepper. Toss until the potatoes are well coated in oil. Arrange the sweet potatoes in a single layer on a baking sheet. Roast for 30 minutes, flipping them halfway through, until they start to brown.

2. Assemble each bowl with half of the arugula, chickpeas, barley, sweet potatoes, cabbage, and avocado. Serve with the dressing.

Matcha-Cashew Dressing

Makes about ½ cup

¼ cup raw cashews, soaked in water for 30 minutes

¼ cup water

1 tablespoon freshly squeezed lemon juice

½ teaspoon matcha green tea powder

Pinch of sea salt

- Rinse and drain the cashews. In a blender, combine the cashews, water, lemon juice, matcha, and salt. Blend on high for about 1 minute, until smooth and creamy, scraping down the sides as needed. Taste and adjust the seasoning, if desired.

INGREDIENTS

2 cups stemmed and chopped kale
1 tablespoon extra-virgin olive oil
2 cups cooked quinoa (page 194)
1 cup cooked chickpeas (page 192)
1 medium avocado, sliced
½ medium lemon, halved
½ cup Beet-Tahini Dressing (recipe follows)

Quinoa Buddha Bowl
with Beet-Tahini Dressing

This bowl appears to be quite basic, but that's because the beet-tahini dressing is the real star here. Roasting the beet and blending it with the other ingredients results in a delectable, creamy dressing that adds punch to anything it accompanies. This dressing also shines in the Roasted Winter Squash & Pomegranate Bowl (page 141), as well as most of the bowls in this section.

Makes 2 bowls

1. In a medium bowl, combine the kale and oil. Massage the kale with the oil for a couple minutes by hand, until tender and shiny.
2. Assemble each bowl with half of the quinoa, chickpeas, kale, and avocado. Garnish with a lemon wedge and serve with the dressing.

Beet-Tahini Dressing

Makes about ½ cup

1 small beet, peeled

¼ cup water

2 tablespoons tahini

1 tablespoon freshly squeezed lemon juice

1 tablespoon extra-virgin olive oil

1 clove garlic, minced

½ teaspoon ground cumin

Pinch of sea salt

- Preheat the oven to 400 degrees F. Wrap the beet in aluminum foil to create a little pouch. Place the pouch on a baking sheet and roast for about 45 minutes, until tender all the way through (stick a toothpick or fork into it to make sure). Remove it from the oven and let cool down before proceeding.
- In a blender, combine the beet, water, tahini, lemon juice, oil, garlic, cumin, and salt. Blend on high for about 1 minute, until smooth and creamy, scraping down the sides as needed. Taste and adjust the seasoning, if desired.

INGREDIENTS

Chipotle-Lime Cauliflower Rice

1 tablespoon avocado oil

2 cups cauliflower rice (page 191) or cooked brown or white rice (page 195)

½ teaspoon chipotle powder

½ teaspoon chili powder

Pinch of sea salt

Pinch of freshly ground black pepper

1 tablespoon minced fresh cilantro

1 tablespoon freshly squeezed lime juice

Pinto Beans

1 tablespoon avocado oil

2 cups cooked pinto beans (page 192)

1 clove garlic, minced

½ teaspoon chili powder

½ teaspoon ground sweet paprika

½ teaspoon ground cumin

¼ teaspoon dried oregano

¼ teaspoon sea salt

¼ teaspoon freshly ground black pepper

2 tablespoons water, plus more as needed

For Serving

1 medium avocado, sliced

2 cups shredded chard

½ medium lime, halved

½ cup Cashew Cheese Dressing (page 103)

Chipotle-Lime Cauliflower Taco Bowl with Cashew Cheese Dressing

This taco bowl is an energizing meal with wholesome ingredients. The chipotle-lime cauliflower rice is reminiscent of the rice that's served in a Mexican restaurant. The cashew cheese makes a delicious plant-based alternative to dairy cheese: the nutritional yeast, which is a complete protein, gives it a "cheesy" flavor along with vitamin B12.

Makes 2 bowls

Continued on next page

1. Prepare the cauliflower rice. In a medium skillet over medium heat, warm the oil. Add the cauliflower rice, chipotle powder, chili powder, salt, and pepper. Stir well and cook for 5 minutes, or until the cauliflower rice is soft. Turn off the heat. Add the cilantro, drizzle with lime juice, and stir well.

2. Prepare the beans. In a small pot over medium heat, warm the oil. Add the pinto beans, garlic, chili powder, paprika, cumin, oregano, salt, and pepper. Stir well and drizzle in the water, adding more if the beans appear dry. Cook for 10 minutes until the spices are fragrant and turn off the heat.

3. Assemble each bowl with half of the cauliflower rice, beans, avocado, and chard. Garnish with a lime wedge and drizzle with the dressing.

INGREDIENTS

Roasted Squash

1 delicata squash, cut into ½-inch-thick slices and seeded

1 tablespoon avocado oil

¼ teaspoon sea salt

¼ teaspoon freshly ground black pepper

Kale Slaw

2 cups kale, stemmed and thinly sliced

1 cup julienned carrot

1 cup shredded red cabbage

¼ cup thinly sliced red onion

1 tablespoon freshly squeezed lemon juice

1 tablespoon extra-virgin olive oil

Pinch of sea salt

Pinch of freshly ground black pepper

For Serving

1 medium avocado, sliced

½ cup Lemon-Tahini Dressing (page 71)

Roasted Delicata Squash & Kale Slaw Bowl with Lemon-Tahini Dressing

Delicata squash is a type of winter heirloom squash with a rich flavor. It's my favorite squash to cook with because it has an edible peel, which makes it so easy to chop and prepare—especially compared to butternut and other varieties. Delicata is also hardy and can be stored for about three months in a dry, cool place. In this bowl, the squash is roasted and served with a vibrant kale slaw. This dish can be enjoyed later without needing to be reheated.

Makes 2 bowls

1. Prepare the squash. Preheat the oven to 425 degrees F. In a medium bowl, toss the squash, avocado oil, salt, and pepper. Arrange in a single layer on a baking sheet. Roast for 25 minutes, or until the squash starts to brown, flipping it halfway through.

2. Prepare the slaw. In a medium bowl, combine the kale, carrot, cabbage, onion, lemon juice, olive oil, salt, and pepper. Mix well.
3. Assemble each bowl with half of the kale slaw, roasted squash, and avocado. Serve with the dressing.

Treat Bowls

Chocolate-Tahini Fudge Ice Cream (page 182)

Eating real food doesn't mean depriving yourself of **sweet treats**. This section is dedicated to offering energy-boosting sweet bowls, including ice creams, that taste delicious but won't leave you with a sugar crash when you're done.

Ice cream played an important role in my childhood, as it does for most kids! It was my favorite treat. When I started cutting down on dairy consumption to help heal my digestive system, I started looking for alternatives. Coconut-milk ice cream is where I landed: it's a great option for those sensitive to dairy.

Due to its high fat content, coconut milk doesn't quite reach the thick consistency that ice cream made from cow's milk does, but what I really like is that it results in a soft-serve texture, which is often difficult to achieve with other plant-based milks. While it helps if you enjoy the taste of coconut, many of the flavorings do a fine job of masking it, with only a hint of coconut flavor in each bite.

If you're not a fan of coconut or don't own an ice-cream maker, there are other recipes included here that can satisfy your sweet tooth, including a smoothie bowl, chia pudding, and bliss balls.

INGREDIENTS

Coconut Chia Pudding

2 cups full-fat coconut milk

¼ cup chia seeds

1 teaspoon vanilla extract

1 teaspoon pure maple syrup

Pinch of sea salt

Caramelized Bananas

2 tablespoons coconut oil

2 bananas, sliced

¼ teaspoon ground cinnamon

Pinch of sea salt

For Serving

2 tablespoons roughly chopped Brazil nuts

2 tablespoons hemp seeds

2 tablespoons almond or peanut butter (page 188)

Coconut Chia Pudding Bowl
with Caramelized Bananas

Chia pudding is a simple, easy-to-make recipe that can be prepared for breakfast, a snack, or dessert. Layering it with sweet caramelized bananas creates an explosion of flavor with every bite. The Brazil nuts add a bit of crunch, healthy fats, and a boost of energy.

Makes 2 bowls

1. Prepare the chia pudding. In a large mason jar, combine the coconut milk, chia seeds, vanilla, maple syrup, and salt. Tightly close the jar and shake for about 30 seconds, or until the ingredients are combined. Let it sit for 3 minutes and give it one more shake. Set the pudding aside to thicken for 30 minutes.

2. Once the pudding has thickened, prepare the caramelized bananas. In a large skillet over medium heat, warm the oil. Place the slices of banana in the pan in a single layer. Sprinkle with cinnamon and salt. Cook for 4 minutes, then flip and cook for another 4 minutes once the bananas start to caramelize and turn golden brown. Turn off the heat.
3. Assemble each bowl with half of the chia pudding, caramelized bananas, Brazil nuts, hemp seeds, and nut butter.

INGREDIENTS

2 sweet potatoes (about 10 ounces)

¼ cup almond or peanut butter (page 188)

2 tablespoons old-fashioned rolled oats or granola

Other toppings of choice: ground cinnamon, shredded coconut, coconut yogurt, cacao nibs, chopped almonds, etc.

Baked Sweet Potato Bowl

with Nut Butter

This baked sweet potato with almond butter is such a simple and delicious treat you won't know whether to eat it for breakfast or dessert! One would never expect the two ingredients to go well hand in hand, but this recipe will leave you pleasantly surprised and satisfied.

Makes 2 bowls

1. Preheat the oven to 400 degrees F. Pierce each sweet potato four to five times with a fork and place them in the oven on a baking sheet. Bake for 30 minutes, or until the sweet potatoes are tender (use a toothpick to test them).
2. Cut each sweet potato in half and let them cool down for a few minutes.
3. Assemble each bowl with one sweet potato and half of the nut butter, oats, and other toppings of your choice.

INGREDIENTS

Bliss Balls

½ cup unsweetened coconut flakes

½ cup raw almonds

¼ cup almond butter (page 188)

¼ cup pepitas

¼ cup hemp seeds

¼ cup raw cashews

¼ cup pitted Medjool dates

¼ cup unsweetened almond milk

2 tablespoons coconut oil, melted

1 tablespoon rosewater

1 teaspoon ground cinnamon

For Serving

2 cups plain coconut yogurt

¼ cup almond butter (page 188)

1 cup blueberries

Rosewater Bliss Ball & Yogurt Bowl

Bliss balls are yummy, easy to transport, and loaded with energy, healthy fats, and so much goodness. They serve as a great pre- or post-workout fuel and keep sweet cravings at bay. The rosewater makes these balls reminiscent of a cooling Indian drink called *rooh afza*.

Makes 2 bowls (plus extra bliss balls)

1. In a food processor, combine the coconut flakes, almonds, almond butter, pepitas, hemp seeds, cashews, dates, almond milk, oil, rosewater, and cinnamon. Pulse for 1 to 2 minutes, until the mixture becomes crumbly. Using a small cookie scoop, divide the mixture into twelve mounds. With your hands, roll each mound into a ball.

2. Assemble each bowl with half of the yogurt, almond butter, and blueberries. Top with 1 or 2 bliss balls.

3. Store the remaining bliss balls in an airtight container at room temperature or in the refrigerator for up to a week.

Note

Feel free to dip the bliss balls in additional toppings, such as coconut flakes, matcha powder, hemp seeds, or ground cinnamon.

INGREDIENTS

2 big handfuls fresh spinach
1 cup diced fresh or frozen mango
1 cup almond milk
½ cup water, plus more as needed
2 tablespoons hemp seeds
1 tablespoon chia seeds
1 teaspoon matcha green tea powder
½ teaspoon minced peeled fresh ginger
2 pitted dates, for added sweetness (optional)

Optional Toppings
¼ cup sliced banana
¼ cup unsweetened coconut flakes
2 tablespoons chopped raw almonds
2 tablespoons nut butter of choice (page 188)
2 tablespoons minced fresh mint

Mango-Ginger Smoothie Bowl

This smoothie bowl is ideal for late spring or all throughout summer when mango is in season. The ginger adds a spicy kick (use more or less than the recipe calls for based on preference), while the mango contributes sweetness. You can add dates for additional sweetness if you'd like. Putting this bowl together takes all of two minutes, especially if you have your mango ready to go! Because of how thick it is, this treat is best served in a bowl topped with additional ingredients. If you prefer to drink the smoothie from a glass, just stir in more water.

Makes 2 bowls

1. In a blender, combine the spinach, mango, almond milk, water, hemp seeds, chia seeds, matcha, ginger, and dates. Blend on high speed for about 2 minutes, until smooth, thick, and creamy.
2. Divide the smoothie between two bowls and garnish each with half of the optional toppings.

INGREDIENTS

Caramelized Bananas

2 tablespoons coconut oil

2 bananas, halved lengthwise

¼ teaspoon ground cinnamon

Pinch of sea salt

For Serving

2 cups plain coconut yogurt

1 cup berries of choice (blueberries, strawberries, raspberries, or blackberries)

½ cup granola (optional)

¼ cup nut butter of choice (page 188)

2 tablespoons raw chopped almonds

2 tablespoons unsweetened coconut flakes

2 tablespoons cacao nibs

1 tablespoon chia seeds

Berry Banana Split Bowl

This bowl is reminiscent of a childhood favorite and reminds me of those warm summer days growing up when I'd share a banana split with my siblings. The caramelized bananas are a tasty companion to the berries and coconut yogurt, while the other toppings will give you an energy kick. Perfect for children and adults alike, this bowl satisfies the sweet tooth in a slightly healthier way.

Makes 2 bowls

1. Prepare the bananas. In a large skillet over medium heat, warm the oil. Place the slices of banana in the pan in a single layer. Sprinkle with cinnamon and sea salt. Cook for 4 minutes, then flip and cook for another 4 minutes until the bananas start to turn golden brown. Turn off the heat.

2. Assemble each bowl with half of the yogurt, warm caramelized bananas, berries, granola, nut butter, almonds, coconut flakes, cacao nibs, and chia seeds.

INGREDIENTS

¼ cup raw cashews, soaked in water for 30 minutes

1 (12-ounce) can full-fat coconut milk

¼ cup pure maple syrup

1 tablespoon coconut oil

1 teaspoon vanilla extract

½-inch piece peeled fresh turmeric, sliced, or ¼ teaspoon ground turmeric

½-inch piece peeled fresh ginger, sliced, or ¼ teaspoon ground ginger

¼ teaspoon ground cardamom

¼ teaspoon ground cinnamon

Pinch of sea salt

Pinch of freshly ground black pepper

Golden Milk Latte Ice Cream

Turmeric (or *haldi* in Hindi) has been used in Indian cuisine for thousands of years. Recently, it's become more popular in other parts of the world as well. Golden milk is a traditional hot Indian beverage made from milk, turmeric, and a combination of other fragrant, healing spices. This simple plant-based version makes for a delectable creamed treat.

Makes 1 quart

1. Freeze the bowl from an ice-cream maker for at least 24 hours before using.
2. Rinse and drain the cashews. In a blender, combine the cashews, coconut milk, maple syrup, oil, vanilla, turmeric, ginger, cardamom, cinnamon, salt, and pepper. Blend on high for 2 to 3 minutes, until smooth and creamy, scraping down the sides as needed.

3. Pour the mixture into a small saucepan and bring to a simmer over low heat. Simmer for 5 minutes, turn off the heat, and let the mixture cool down. Strain through a fine-mesh sieve into a lidded container and refrigerate for a few hours, until completely cool, before churning.

4. Following the ice-cream maker's instructions, churn the ice cream until it resembles soft serve. Transfer to an airtight container, place a sheet of parchment paper on the surface, and freeze for at least 1 hour before serving.

Note

Since turmeric is so powerful, a small amount goes a long way. It also stains everything it touches, so use it with care. If you spill any of the ice-cream mixture on your countertop, be sure to wipe it up immediately.

INGREDIENTS

2 cups fresh blackberries

¼ cup raw cashews, soaked in water for 30 minutes

1 (12-ounce) can full-fat coconut milk

¼ cup pure maple syrup or other sweetener of choice

1 tablespoon coconut oil

½ teaspoon dried lavender flowers

2 tablespoons freshly squeezed lemon juice

Pinch of sea salt

Blackberry-Lavender Ice Cream

Blackberries and summer go hand in hand. Here, the tartness of the berries balances the maple-coconut sweetness of this refreshing ice cream. Berries pair deliciously with floral flavors, especially lavender. The taste is reminiscent of taking a walk on a cool summer night. If you like, you can swap blueberries for the blackberries.

Makes 1 quart

1. Freeze the bowl from an ice-cream maker for at least 24 hours before using.
2. In a blender or food processor, puree the blackberries. Strain through a fine-mesh sieve into a bowl. Discard the pulp and seeds.
3. Rinse and drain the cashews. In a blender, combine the blackberries, cashews, coconut milk, maple syrup, oil, lavender, lemon juice, and salt. Blend on high for 1 minute, until smooth and creamy, scraping down the sides as needed.
4. Pour the mixture into a small saucepan and bring to a simmer over low heat. Simmer for 5 minutes, turn off the heat, and let the mixture cool down.

5. Pour the mixture into a lidded container and refrigerate for a few hours, until completely cool, before churning.
6. Following the ice-cream maker's instructions, churn the ice cream until it resembles soft serve. Transfer to an airtight container, place a sheet of parchment paper on the surface, and freeze for at least 1 hour before serving.

Notes

- If you can't find lavender flowers, substitute a drop of food-grade lavender essential oil.
- If you're using a high-speed blender, it won't be necessary to discard the blackberry pulp, as the berries will be fully pulverized.

Note

You can purchase activated charcoal from your local natural food store. Open up a single capsule and empty the contents until you have the amount needed.

INGREDIENTS

¼ cup pitted Medjool dates, soaked in water for 30 minutes

¼ cup raw cashews, soaked in water for 30 minutes

1 (12-ounce) can full-fat coconut milk

1 tablespoon coconut oil

¼ teaspoon food-grade activated charcoal

Juice from 1½ medium lemons (about 3 tablespoons)

Pinch of sea salt

Ash-Lemon Ice Cream

This ice cream is tangy and refreshingly delicious, plus it comes with some potential health benefits. Activated charcoal is what gives this treat its ash-like hue, and it allegedly has a cleansing effect on the body, acting like a magnet for toxins.

Makes 1 quart

1. Freeze the bowl from an ice-cream maker for at least 24 hours before using.
2. Rinse and drain the dates and cashews. In a blender, combine the dates, cashews, coconut milk, oil, charcoal, lemon juice, and salt. Blend on high for 1 minute, until smooth and creamy, scraping down the sides as needed.
3. Pour the mixture into a small saucepan and bring to a simmer over low heat. Simmer for 5 minutes, turn off the heat, and let the mixture cool down. Strain through a fine-mesh sieve into a lidded container and refrigerate for a few hours, until completely cool, before churning.
4. Following the ice-cream maker's instructions, churn the ice cream until it resembles soft serve. Transfer to an airtight container, place a sheet of parchment paper on the surface, and freeze for at least 1 hour before serving.

INGREDIENTS

½ cup pitted Medjool dates, soaked in water for 30 minutes

1 (12-ounce) can full-fat coconut milk

¼ cup tahini

3 tablespoons cocoa powder or cacao powder

1 tablespoon coconut oil

1 teaspoon vanilla extract, or ¼ teaspoon vanilla bean powder

Pinch of sea salt

Chocolate-Tahini Fudge Ice Cream

The combination of cocoa powder and tahini creates a smooth and luscious treat—think a rich, somewhat buttery fudge. Tahini is made from ground sesame seeds and has vitamins, calcium, minerals, and other nutritional benefits. To up the health ante, use cacao powder, which is less processed and contains more antioxidants than cocoa. Top the ice cream with fresh berries to elevate the flavor or sesame seeds to add a little crunch.

Makes 1 quart

1. Freeze the bowl from an ice-cream maker for at least 24 hours before using.
2. Rinse and drain the dates. In a blender, combine the dates, coconut milk, tahini, cocoa powder, oil, vanilla, and salt. Blend on high for 1 minute, until smooth and creamy, scraping down the sides as needed.
3. Pour the mixture into a small saucepan and bring to a simmer over low heat. Simmer for 5 minutes, turn off the heat, and let the mixture cool down.

4. Strain through a fine-mesh sieve into a lidded container and refrigerate for a few hours, until completely cool, before churning.
5. Following the ice-cream maker's instructions, churn the ice cream until it resembles soft serve. Transfer to an airtight container, place a sheet of parchment paper on the surface, and freeze for at least 1 hour before serving.

INGREDIENTS

¼ cup raw cashews, soaked in water for 30 minutes

1 (12-ounce) can full-fat coconut milk

2 cups fresh or frozen strawberries

½ teaspoon grated peeled fresh ginger

¼ cup pure maple syrup

1 tablespoon coconut oil

1 teaspoon vanilla extract, or seeds scraped from ½ vanilla bean

Juice from ½ medium lemon (about 1 tablespoon)

Pinch of sea salt

Strawberry-Ginger Ice Cream

Strawberries were one of my favorite fruits growing up. Ginger was not something I started enjoying until a few years ago, but I quickly learned that the two work well together to create a zingy strawberry treat with a hint of heat. Depending on how spicy you want this ice cream to be, feel free to double or halve the suggested amount of ginger. I suggest purchasing organic strawberries to use here since conventional options are notorious for containing pesticide residue.

Makes 1 quart

1. Freeze the bowl from an ice-cream maker for at least 24 hours before using.

2. Rinse and drain the cashews. In a blender, combine the cashews, coconut milk, strawberries, ginger, maple syrup, oil, vanilla, lemon juice, and salt. Blend on high for 2 to 3 minutes, until smooth and creamy, scraping down the sides as needed.

3. Pour the mixture into a small saucepan and bring to a simmer over low heat. Simmer for 5 minutes, turn off the heat, and let the mixture cool

down. Strain through a fine-mesh sieve into a lidded container and refrigerate for a few hours, until completely cool, before churning.

4. Following the ice-cream maker's instructions, churn the ice cream until it resembles soft serve. Transfer to an airtight container, place a sheet of parchment paper on the surface, and freeze for at least 1 hour before serving.

STAUB

Basic How-To Recipes

When I first started cooking, I decided I was okay with paying a little more for convenience. This included buying canned beans, tomato sauces, and much more. But as I became confident with my cooking skills, I realized how much cheaper it is to make your own. Often it doesn't take too much extra work, either. You can prepare big batches of quinoa and beans over the weekend, for example, and keep them in the fridge for several days for easy use throughout the week. This chapter contains all of the master batch-cooking preparations you'll need to make your plant power bowls—from cauliflower rice to tahini.

INGREDIENTS

3 cups raw almonds or raw unsalted peanuts

¼ teaspoon sea salt

Nut Butter

Making your own creamy almond or peanut butter is easy and convenient—all you need are the nuts and a high-speed blender or food processor. To save even more time, you can purchase dry-roasted nuts and proceed to step three. Cleanup can get a little messy, but then again, you have an excuse to lick the spatula.

Makes about 1½ cups

1. Preheat the oven to 375 degrees F and line a baking sheet with parchment paper.
2. Spread the nuts in a single layer on the baking sheet and roast for 10 minutes, or until lightly browned. Let the nuts cool before blending.
3. Transfer the nuts to a high-speed blender or food processor. Blend for about 10 minutes, scraping the sides frequently with a spatula, until smooth and creamy. Add the salt and blend for another minute to incorporate.
4. Pour the butter into an airtight container and store in the refrigerator for up to 2 to 3 weeks.

INGREDIENTS

2 cups hulled sesame seeds

¼ cup avocado oil or extra-virgin olive oil

Tahini

If you have trouble finding tahini at the store, it's very easy to make your own at home with sesame seeds, oil, and a high-speed blender or food processor. Using hulled sesame seeds will make the tahini smoother and less bitter.

Makes about 2 cups

1. In a medium saucepan over low heat, toast the sesame seeds for a few minutes, stirring frequently. Once the seeds are fragrant and start to turn slightly golden, turn off the heat.
2. Transfer the sesame seeds to a high-speed blender or food processor. Blend on high for 8 to 10 minutes, scraping the sides frequently with a spatula, until they create a paste. Drizzle in the oil and continue to blend on high for 3 to 4 minutes, until the tahini is smooth and creamy.
3. Pour the tahini into an airtight container and store in the refrigerator for up to 4 weeks. If the tahini starts to separate, stir well to reincorporate.

INGREDIENTS

2 cups cooked chickpeas (page 192)

¼ cup extra-virgin olive oil or avocado oil, plus more for drizzling

2 tablespoons tahini

2 tablespoons freshly squeezed lemon juice

1 clove garlic, minced

¼ teaspoon sea salt

Hummus

Hummus is the first dip I learned how to make when I started cooking at home on a regular basis. I discovered it was so much easier to make than it seemed. It tastes much better than most options you can purchase from a grocery store, and it takes no time at all: you can whip up a batch in less than five minutes.

Makes about 2 cups

1. In a food processor, combine the chickpeas, oil, tahini, lemon juice, garlic, and salt. Blend for 3 to 4 minutes, scraping the sides with a spatula, until the hummus is smooth and creamy.
2. Scoop the hummus into a dish and drizzle with additional oil. If you'd like to store it, transfer to an airtight container and store in the refrigerator for 3 to 4 days.

INGREDIENTS

1 head cauliflower, cut into florets

Cauliflower Rice

Cauliflower rice is all the rage these days and can be purchased inexpensively (frozen or fresh) at many grocery stores, saving you a little time in the kitchen—though it hardly takes much time from scratch. If you don't have a food processor, cut the cauliflower into bigger pieces and use a grater instead; just be careful not to hurt yourself.

Makes 4 to 5 cups, depending on size of the cauliflower

1. In a food processor, pulse the cauliflower until the texture resembles rice. Alternatively, you can use the shredder attachment and run the cauliflower florets through the feed tube.
2. Store in an airtight container in the refrigerator for up to 3 days or in the freezer for up to 2 months.

INGREDIENTS

1 cup dried black, pinto, or cannellini beans, or chickpeas

About 4 cups water, for cooking

Beans

The ratio of this basic recipe applies to chickpeas and essentially all kinds of dried beans, including black, pinto, and cannellini. If you'd like to insert a little more flavor during cooking, feel free to use vegetable stock in place of water, but wait to season with any salt until after the beans are fully cooked, or they will get tough. I normally pick one or two beans to prep on Sunday or Monday, and then use them throughout the week.

Makes 2 to 4 cups, depending on type of bean

1. In a large bowl, soak the beans in water for 8 hours or overnight. When ready to cook, rinse well.

2. Place the beans in a medium saucepan and add enough water to cover them by about 2 inches.

3. Bring the water to a boil, then reduce the heat to maintain a simmer. Simmer for about 1 hour, until the beans are tender, adding more water as needed. Drain any excess water.

4. Once the beans have cooled, store them in an airtight container in the refrigerator for up to 3 days.

INGREDIENTS

1 cup dried green or brown lentils
About 4 cups water, for cooking
Pinch of sea salt

Lentils

Compared to many other legumes, lentils are quick and easy to prepare. They also absorb flavor from other ingredients more readily. It's not necessary to soak lentils as it is with dried beans, but if you'd like to soak them, a few hours is plenty; rinse them well before proceeding with cooking.

Makes 2½ cups

1. Rinse and drain the lentils.
2. Place the lentils in a medium saucepan and add enough water to cover them by about 2 inches.
3. Bring the water to a boil, then reduce the heat to maintain a simmer. Simmer for about 45 minutes, until the lentils are tender, adding more water as needed. Drain any excess water and add the salt.
4. Once the lentils have cooled down, store in an airtight container in the refrigerator for up to 5 days.

Grains

Adding grains (and pseudo-grains, such as quinoa and buckwheat) is a versatile way to make your bowls more filling. Cooking your own grains is a much more affordable option than buying them at the store, and it's simple to add this prep into a weekly routine. It also ensures you're using a cleaner product with minimal ingredients. The recipes outlined in the following pages are very basic, so you may want to consider adding an aromatic or herb to the water if you're feeling more adventurous!

Quinoa

Makes 3 cups

1 cup quinoa
2 cups water
Pinch of sea salt

- Rinse the quinoa in a fine-mesh sieve and drain.
- In a medium pot, combine the quinoa, water, and salt.
- Bring the water to a boil. Reduce the heat to low and cover tightly.
- After 5 minutes, turn off the heat and let the steam finish cooking the quinoa until all of the water is absorbed (don't remove the lid!), about 20 minutes.
- Fluff the quinoa with a fork. Store in an airtight container in the refrigerator for up to a week.

White or Basmati Rice

Makes 3 cups

1 cup rice
2 cups water
Pinch of sea salt

- Rinse the rice in a fine-mesh sieve and drain.
- In a medium pot, combine the rice, water, and salt.
- Bring the water to a boil, then reduce the heat to maintain a simmer. Simmer for 5 minutes and turn off the heat.
- Cover tightly and let the steam cook the rice for about 20 minutes, until the water is absorbed and the rice is tender. Store in an airtight container in the refrigerator for up to 3 days.

Brown Rice

Makes 3 cups

1 cup brown rice
2 cups water
Pinch of sea salt

- Rinse the rice in a fine-mesh sieve and drain.
- In a medium pot, combine the rice, water, and salt.
- Bring the water to a boil, then reduce the heat to maintain a simmer.
- Cover tightly and cook for 30 to 40 minutes, until the water is absorbed and the rice is tender. Store in an airtight container in the refrigerator for up to 3 days.

Millet

Makes 4 cups

1 cup millet
2 cups water
Pinch of sea salt

- Rinse the millet in a fine-mesh sieve and drain.
- In a medium pot, combine the millet, water, and salt.
- Bring the water to a boil, cover with a lid, and reduce the heat to maintain a simmer.
- Simmer for about 20 minutes, until the water is absorbed and millet is tender.
- Fluff the millet with a fork. Store in an airtight container in the refrigerator for up to 3 days.

Pearl Barley

Makes 3½ cups

1 cup pearl barley
2 ½ cups water
1 tablespoon avocado oil
1 teaspoon sea salt

- Rinse the barley in a fine-mesh sieve and drain.
- In a medium pot, combine the barley, water, oil, and salt.
- Bring the water to a boil, then reduce the heat to maintain a simmer. Simmer for 5 minutes and turn off the heat.
- Cover tightly and let it sit until the water is absorbed, about 50 minutes. Store in an airtight container in the refrigerator for up to 3 days.

Buckwheat

Makes 4 cups

1 cup buckwheat groats
2 cups water
Pinch of sea salt

- Rinse the buckwheat in a fine-mesh sieve and drain.
- Heat a medium saucepan over medium-high heat. Add the buckwheat and toast for about 2 minutes, stirring frequently, until fragrant.
- Add the water and salt and bring to a boil. Reduce the heat to maintain a simmer and cover tightly. Cook for about 10 minutes, until the buckwheat is tender. Drain any excess water.
- Store in an airtight container in the refrigerator for up to 3 days.

Farro

Makes 3 cups

1 cup farro
3 cups water
Pinch of sea salt

- Rinse the farro in a fine-mesh sieve and drain.
- Heat a medium saucepan over medium heat. Add the farro and toast for about 2 minutes, stirring frequently, until fragrant.
- Add the water and salt and bring to a boil. Reduce the heat to maintain a simmer and cover tightly. Cook for 20 to 30 minutes, until the farro is tender. Drain any excess water.
- Store in an airtight container in the refrigerator for up to 3 days.

Gratitude & Acknowledgments

No one writes a book alone. We all need support through the ups and downs, from the beginning to the end, especially in the moments we want to give up because we don't think we can do it. Writing this book has truly been an unforgettable journey. And it wouldn't have been possible without a lot of love and support.

I am grateful to the incredible team at Sasquatch Books. Susan Roxborough, thank you so much for this opportunity, for your support and guidance. Rachelle Longé McGhee, thank you for all your hard work—you are truly incredible and so talented. Thank you, Bryce de Flamand, you are amazing and such a joy to work with. Thank you also, Daniel Germain and Anna Goldstein, for all your guidance and support!

I'm so grateful to my sweet and loving family, who has been my biggest support system and so encouraging through this entire journey. Thank you, Mom and Dad, for teaching me about the importance of health and real food well before I ever realized it.

Kerri Roberts, Krissy Simon, and Shalini Wilfred—thank you from the bottom of my heart for being my rocks. Thank you, David Em, for my portraits and endless help on the art of editing. I have so much gratitude to my team of recipe testers, whose feedback was so important in making each recipe shine. Thank you for your time, energy, and support.

Thank you to anyone who's touched my life in any way during this beautiful journey. And most importantly, thank you to my *Real + Vibrant* community. I am forever grateful to you. You are my motivation, strength, and inspiration. This book and its recipes are for you.

Index

Note: Page numbers in *italic* refer to photographs.

D

E

F

G

H

I